# LIFE'S LITTLE BOOK OF
# WISDOM FOR
# *Mothers*

© 2008 by Barbour Publishing, Inc.

ISBN 978-1-59789-955-0

Published by Barbour Publishing, Inc., P.O. Box 719, Uhrichsville, Ohio 44683, www.barbourbooks.com

*Our mission is to publish and distribute inspirational products offering exceptional value and biblical encouragement to the masses.*

Printed in China.

# LIFE'S LITTLE BOOK OF
## WISDOM FOR
*Mothers*

BARBOUR
PUBLISHING

*A mother's love perceives no impossibilities.*

CORNELIA PADDOCK

You will find as you look back upon your life that the moments when you have truly lived are the moments when you have done things in the spirit of love.

Henry Drummond

BE THE LIVING EXPRESSION OF GOD'S KINDNESS:
KINDNESS IN YOUR FACE,
KINDNESS IN YOUR EYES,
KINDNESS IN YOUR SMILE.

MOTHER TERESA

*So much of what we know of love we learn from home.*

UNKNOWN

BECOMING A MOTHER MAKES YOU THE
MOTHER OF ALL CHILDREN. YOU LONG TO
COMFORT ALL WHO ARE DESOLATE.

CHARLOTTE GRAY

*Children are a gift from the Lord;*
*they are a reward from him.*

PSALM 127:3 NLT

A MOTHER'S HAPPINESS IS LIKE A BEACON,
LIGHTING UP THE FUTURE BUT REFLECTED ALSO
ON THE PAST IN THE GUISE OF FOND MEMORIES.

HONORÉ DE BALZAC

THE MOTHER IS AND MUST BE—WHETHER SHE
KNOWS IT OR NOT—THE GREATEST, STRONGEST,
AND MOST LASTING TEACHER HER CHILDREN HAVE.

HANNAH WHITALL SMITH

Through the ages no nation has had a better friend than the mother who taught her child to pray.

Unknown

The mother love is like God's love;
He loves us not because we are lovable,
but because it is His nature to love,
and because we are His children.

Earl Riney

CHILDREN ARE WHAT THE MOTHERS ARE.
NO FATHER'S FONDEST CARE CAN
FASHION SO THE INFANT HEART.

W. S. LANDOR

*The mother's heart is the child's schoolroom.*

Henry Ward Beecher

CHARM IS DECEPTIVE, AND BEAUTY IS
FLEETING; BUT A WOMAN WHO FEARS
THE LORD IS TO BE PRAISED.

PROVERBS 31:30 NIV

THERE ARE ONLY TWO LASTING BEQUESTS
WE CAN HOPE TO GIVE OUR CHILDREN.
ONE IS ROOTS; AND THE OTHER, WINGS.

HODDING CARTER

To be a mother is a
woman's greatest vocation in life.
She is a partner with God.

SPENCER W. KIMBALL

*There is no influence so powerful as that of the mother.*

SARAH JOSEPHA HALE

HER DIGNITY CONSISTS IN
BEING UNKNOWN TO THE WORLD;
HER GLORY IS IN THE ESTEEM OF HER HUSBAND;
HER PLEASURES IN THE HAPPINESS OF HER FAMILY.

JEAN-JACQUES ROUSSEAU

WHERE YOUR PLEASURE IS, THERE IS YOUR TREASURE;
WHERE YOUR TREASURE, THERE YOUR HEART;
WHERE YOUR HEART, THERE YOUR HAPPINESS.

ST. AUGUSTINE

*To give without any reward,
or any notice, has a special
quality of its own.*

ANNE MORROW LINDBERGH

*A child needs a mother more than all the things money can buy.*

EZRA TAFT BENSON

POINT YOUR KIDS IN THE RIGHT DIRECTION—
WHEN THEY'RE OLD THEY WON'T BE LOST.

PROVERBS 22:6 MSG

*The imprint of the mother remains forever on the life of the child.*

UNKNOWN

THE POWER OF ONE MOTHER'S PRAYERS
COULD STAND AN ARMY ON ITS EAR.

ELIZABETH DEHAVEN

*Maternal love:*
*a miraculous substance which*
*God multiplies as He divides it.*

Victor Hugo

NEVER DESPAIR OF A CHILD.
THE ONE YOU WEEP THE MOST FOR
AT THE MERCY-SEAT MAY FILL YOUR
HEART WITH THE SWEETEST JOYS.

T. L. CUYLER

*Love comes when we
take the time to understand
and care for another person.*

JANETTE OKE

GOD PARDONS LIKE A MOTHER,
WHO KISSES THE OFFENSE INTO
EVERLASTING FORGIVENESS.

HENRY WARD BEECHER

BE AN EXAMPLE TO ALL BELIEVERS IN
WHAT YOU SAY, IN THE WAY YOU LIVE,
IN YOUR LOVE, YOUR FAITH, AND YOUR PURITY.

1 TIMOTHY 4:12 NLT

When I come to the end of my rope,
God is there to take over.

UNKNOWN

It is not our exalted feelings, it is our sentiments that build the necessary home.

Elizabeth Bowen

*Other things may change us,*
*but we start and end with the family.*

ANTHONY BRANDT

*When there's love at home,*
*there is beauty all around.*

UNKNOWN

THE CONSCIOUSNESS OF CHILDREN
IS FORMED BY THE INFLUENCES THAT
SURROUND THEM; THEIR NOTIONS OF
GOOD AND EVIL ARE THE RESULT OF THE
MORAL ATMOSPHERE THEY BREATHE.

JEAN PAUL RICHTER

THE MOTHER LOVES HER CHILD MOST DIVINELY,
NOT WHEN SHE SURROUNDS HIM WITH COMFORT
AND ANTICIPATES HIS WANTS, BUT WHEN SHE
RESOLUTELY HOLDS HIM TO THE HIGHEST
STANDARDS AND IS CONTENT WITH
NOTHING LESS THAN HIS BEST.

HAMILTON WRIGHT MABIE

THE MOST IMPORTANT PIECE OF
CLOTHING YOU MUST WEAR IS LOVE.
LOVE IS WHAT BINDS US ALL TOGETHER
IN PERFECT HARMONY.

COLOSSIANS 3:14 NLT

*Motherhood is a partnership with God.*

UNKNOWN

MOTHERS HAVE AS POWERFUL AN INFLUENCE
OVER THE WELFARE OF FUTURE GENERATIONS
AS ALL OTHER CAUSES COMBINED.

JOHN ABBOTT

I HAVE HELD MANY THINGS IN MY HANDS
AND I HAVE LOST THEM ALL; BUT WHATEVER
I HAVE PLACED IN GOD'S HANDS,
THAT I STILL POSSESS.

MARTIN LUTHER

*There was never a great man
who had not a great mother.*

OLIVE SCHREINER

*Duty makes us do things well,*
*but love makes us do them beautifully.*

PHILLIPS BROOKS

WHEN YOU LEAD YOUR SONS AND
DAUGHTERS IN THE GOOD WAY, LET YOUR
WORDS BE TENDER AND CARESSING, IN TERMS
OF DISCIPLINE THAT WINS THE HEART'S ASSENT.

ELIJAH BEN SOLOMON ZALMAN

The joy of the Lord
is your strength.

NEHEMIAH 8:10 KJV

THERE IS NO DOUBT THAT IT IS AROUND
THE FAMILY AND THE HOME THAT ALL THE
GREATEST VIRTUES, THE MOST DOMINATING
VIRTUES OF HUMAN SOCIETY, ARE CREATED,
STRENGTHENED, AND MAINTAINED.

WINSTON CHURCHILL

*Many make the household,*
*but only one the home.*

JAMES RUSSELL LOWELL

LOVE BEGINS BY TAKING CARE OF
THE CLOSEST ONES—THE ONES AT HOME.

MOTHER TERESA

*The great doing of little things
makes the great life.*

EUGENIA PRICE

A HOUSE IS BUILT OF LOGS AND STONE,
OF TILES AND POSTS AND PIERS;
A HOME IS BUILT OF LOVING DEEDS
THAT STAND A THOUSAND YEARS.

VICTOR HUGO

*The hardest job you'll ever love is being a mother.*

UNKNOWN

THOSE WHO SOW IN TEARS
WILL REAP WITH SONGS OF JOY.

PSALM 126:5 NIV

*What the heart has once owned,*
*it shall never lose.*

HENRY WARD BEECHER

I DO NOT LOVE HIM BECAUSE HE IS GOOD.
I LOVE HIM BECAUSE HE IS MY CHILD.

RABINDRANATH TAGORE

*How vast a memory has Love!*

ALEXANDER POPE

A MOTHER'S LOVE IS LIKE A CIRCLE.
IT HAS NO BEGINNING AND NO ENDING.
IT KEEPS GOING AROUND AND AROUND,
EVER EXPANDING, TOUCHING EVERYONE
WHO COMES IN CONTACT WITH IT.

UNKNOWN

*Mother's love grows by giving.*

CHARLES LAMB

HAPPINESS CONSISTS MORE IN SMALL
CONVENIENCES OR PLEASURES THAT
OCCUR EVERY DAY THAN IN GREAT
PIECES OF GOOD FORTUNE.

BENJAMIN FRANKLIN

There is nothing so strong as the force of love; there is no love so forcible as the love of an affectionate mother to her child.

ELIZABETH GRYMESTON

"When a woman gives birth, she has a hard time, there's no getting around it. But when the baby is born, there is joy in the birth. This new life in the world wipes out memory of the pain."

John 16:21 msg

A MOTHER LAUGHS OUR LAUGHS, SHEDS OUR
TEARS, RETURNS OUR LOVE, FEARS OUR FEARS.
SHE LIVES OUR JOYS, CARES OUR CARES,
AND ALL OUR HOPES AND DREAMS SHE SHARES.

UNKNOWN

*It is better to have nobility of character than nobility of birth.*

JEWISH PROVERB

THE MOTHER IS EVERYTHING—SHE IS OUR
CONSOLATION IN SORROW, OUR HOPE IN
MISERY, AND OUR STRENGTH IN WEAKNESS.
SHE IS THE SOURCE OF LOVE, MERCY,
SYMPATHY, AND FORGIVENESS.

KAHLIL GIBRAN

The consciousness of loving and being loved brings a warmth and richness to life that nothing else can bring.

OSCAR WILDE

THE FAMILY IS THE ONLY INSTITUTION
IN THE WORLD WHERE THE KINGDOM
OF GOD CAN ACTUALLY BEGIN.

PLATO

*Enjoy the little things,
for one day you may look back
and discover they were the big things.*

UNKNOWN

ONLY A MOTHER KNOWS A MOTHER'S FONDNESS.

LADY MARY WORTLEY MONTAGU

*A happy child has a joyful mother.*

WANDA E. BRUNSTETTER

*Faith is being sure of what we hope for and certain of what we do not see.*

HEBREWS 11:1 NIV

A MOTHER. . .WILL CLING TO US,
AND ENDEAVOR BY HER KIND PRECEPTS
AND COUNSELS TO DISSIPATE THE CLOUDS
OF DARKNESS, AND CAUSE PEACE
TO RETURN TO OUR HEARTS.

WASHINGTON IRVING

NO ORDINARY WORK DONE BY A MAN IS
EITHER AS HARD OR AS RESPONSIBLE AS THE
WORK OF A WOMAN WHO IS BRINGING
UP A FAMILY OF SMALL CHILDREN.

THEODORE ROOSEVELT

*God puts each fresh morning,*
*each new chance of life, into our hands*
*as a gift to see what we will do with it.*

Unknown

*Your greatest pleasure is that
which rebounds from hearts
that you have made glad.*

HENRY WARD BEECHER

THE CHRISTIAN HOME IS THE MASTER'S
WORKSHOP WHERE THE PROCESSES OF
CHARACTER-MOLDING ARE SILENTLY, LOVINGLY,
FAITHFULLY, AND SUCCESSFULLY CARRIED ON.

RICHARD MONCKTON MILNES

SAY TO MOTHERS WHAT A HOLY CHARGE
IS THEIRS. WITH WHAT A KINGLY POWER
THEIR LOVE MIGHT RULE THE FOUNTAINS
OF THE NEWBORN MIND.

LYDIA H. SIGOURNEY

*Nothing is so strong as gentleness.*

ST. FRANCIS DE SALES

*Discipline your son,*
*and he will give you peace;*
*he will bring delight to your soul.*

PROVERBS 29:17 NIV

To laugh often and love much;
To win the respect of intelligent
people and the affection of children. . .
To appreciate beauty; to find the best
in others. . . To know even one life has
breathed easier because you have lived.
That is to have succeeded.

Ralph Waldo Emerson

*Mother—in this consists the glory and the most precious ornament of woman.*

MARTIN LUTHER

A MOTHER'S LOVE AND PRAYERS AND
TEARS ARE SELDOM LOST ON EVEN
THE MOST WAYWARD CHILD.

A. E. DAVIS

*True serenity comes when
we give ourselves to God.*

ELLYN SANNA

THE BURDEN OF LIFE IS FROM OURSELVES,
ITS LIGHTNESS FROM THE GRACE OF
CHRIST AND THE LOVE OF GOD.

WILLIAM B. ULLATHORNE

JUST AS THERE COMES A WARM
SUNBEAM INTO EVERY COTTAGE WINDOW,
SO COMES A LOVEBEAM OF GOD'S CARE
AND PITY FOR EVERY SEPARATE NEED.

NATHANIEL HAWTHORNE

*Grace. . .like the Lord, the giver,*
*never fails from age to age.*

JOHN NEWTON

*The only thing that counts is faith expressing itself through love.*

GALATIANS 5:6 NIV

A MOTHER IS THE ONE THROUGH WHOM
GOD WHISPERS LOVE TO HIS LITTLE CHILDREN.

UNKNOWN

ONE OF GOD'S RICHEST BLESSINGS. . .
IS THAT OUR CHILDREN COME INTO THE
WORLD AS PEOPLE WE'RE SUPPOSED TO GUIDE
AND DIRECT, AND THEN GOD USES THEM
TO FORM US—IF WE WILL ONLY LISTEN.

DENA DYER

*Where we love is home,*
*home that our feet may leave,*
*but not our hearts.*

OLIVER WENDELL HOLMES

CHIDREN ARE A BLESSING
SENT FROM HEAVEN ABOVE,
A HUGGABLE REMINDER
OF GOD'S UNFAILING LOVE.

UNKNOWN

THERE IS NOTHING BUT GOD'S GRACE.
WE WALK UPON IT; WE BREATHE IT;
WE LIVE AND DIE BY IT; IT MAKES THE
NAILS AND AXLES OF THE UNIVERSE.

ROBERT LOUIS STEVENSON

*Children are the anchors
that hold a mother to life.*

SOPHOCLES

LOVE SPENDS ALL, AND STILL HATH STORE.

PHILIP JAMES BAILEY

*Lord, through all the generations
you have been our home!*

PSALM 90:1 NLT

IT IS NOT TRUE THAT LOVE MAKES ALL THINGS EASY;
IT MAKES US CHOOSE WHAT IS DIFFICULT.

GEORGE ELIOT

*If you want to be listened to,*
*you should put in time listening.*

MARGE PIERCY

NO PESSIMIST EVER DISCOVERED THE SECRETS OF THE STARS, OR SAILED TO AN UNCHARTED LAND, OR OPENED A NEW HEAVEN TO THE HUMAN SPIRIT.

HELEN KELLER

*A child is a rare book of which but only one copy is made.*

Unknown

TRUE SILENCE IS THE REST OF THE MIND;
IT IS TO THE SPIRIT WHAT SLEEP IS TO THE
BODY, NOURISHMENT AND REFRESHMENT.

WILLIAM PENN

WHEN YOU GET INTO A TIGHT PLACE
AND EVERYTHING GOES AGAINST YOU,
TILL IT SEEMS AS THOUGH YOU COULD NOT HANG
ON A MINUTE LONGER, NEVER GIVE UP THEN,
FOR THAT IS JUST THE PLACE AND
TIME THAT THE TIDE WILL TURN.

HARRIET BEECHER STOWE

LOVE IS PATIENT, LOVE IS KIND.
IT DOES NOT ENVY, IT DOES NOT
BOAST, IT IS NOT PROUD.

1 CORINTHIANS 13:4 NIV

The nurse of full-grown
souls is solitude.

JAMES RUSSELL LOWELL

I DISCOVERED I ALWAYS HAVE
CHOICES AND SOMETIMES IT'S ONLY
A CHOICE OF ATTITUDE.

JUDITH M. KNOWLTON

*Children don't care what you think
until they think you care.*

UNKNOWN

PARENTS MUST RESPECT THE
SPIRITUAL PERSON OF THEIR CHILD
AND APPROACH IT WITH REVERENCE.

GEORGE MACDONALD

CRITICISM SPEAKS TO THE FAULT WITH THE PERSON;
LOVE SPEAKS TO THE PERSON BEHIND THE FAULT.

HENRY JAMES BORYS

*Love and faithfulness
always breed confidence.*

ST. FRANCIS DE SALES

A MOTHER'S LOVE IS THE HEART
OF THE HOME. HER CHILDREN'S SENSE OF
SECURITY AND SELF-WORTH IS FOUND THERE.

UNKNOWN

COMMIT TO THE LORD WHATEVER YOU DO,
AND YOUR PLANS WILL SUCCEED.

PROVERBS 16:3 NIV

THE PERSON WHO HAS STOPPED BEING
THANKFUL HAS FALLEN ASLEEP IN LIFE.

ROBERT LOUIS STEVENSON

*The present time is the most precious.*

THOMAS à KEMPIS

There is an enduring tenderness in the love
of a mother to a child that transcends
all other affections of the heart.

Washington Irving

BRING LOVE INTO YOUR HOME, FOR THIS IS
WHERE OUR LOVE FOR EACH OTHER MUST START.

MOTHER TERESA

*God gives us love;*
*something to love*
*He lends us.*

ALFRED, LORD TENNYSON

LIVE AS IF EVERYTHING YOU DO
WILL EVENTUALLY BE KNOWN.

HUGH PRATHER

HAPPINESS IS ESSENTIALLY
A STATE OF GOING SOMEWHERE,
WHOLEHEARTEDLY, ONE-DIRECTIONALLY,
WITHOUT REGRET OR RESERVATION.

WILLIAM H. SHELDON

*Love each other as if your
life depended on it. Love makes
up for practically anything.*

1 Peter 4:8 msg

HAVE PATIENCE WITH ALL THINGS,
BUT CHIEFLY HAVE PATIENCE WITH YOURSELF.

ST. FRANCIS DE SALES

To make ourselves happy,
we must make others happy.

CHARLES H. SPURGEON

*It is a special gift to be able to view the world through the eyes of a child.*

UNKNOWN

WORRY NEVER ROBS TOMORROW OF ITS SORROW;
IT ONLY SAPS TODAY OF ITS STRENGTH.

A. J. CRONIN

Do not lose courage in considering
your imperfections, but instantly
set about remedying them—
every day begin the task anew.

St. Francis de Sales

*To dream of the person you would like to be is to waste the person you are.*

UNKNOWN

*Do what you can,
with what you have,
where you are.*

THEODORE ROOSEVELT

THE OLDER WOMEN. . .
CAN TRAIN THE YOUNGER WOMEN TO
LOVE THEIR HUSBANDS AND CHILDREN,
TO BE SELF-CONTROLLED AND PURE,
TO BE BUSY AT HOME, TO BE KIND. . . .

TITUS 2:3-5 NIV

FAMILIES GIVE US MANY THINGS—
LOVE AND MEANING, PURPOSE AND AN
OPPORTUNITY TO GIVE, AND A SENSE OF HUMOR.

UNKNOWN

*A rich child often sits
in a poor mother's lap.*

DANISH PROVERB

The Bible does not say very much about homes;
it says a great deal about the things that
make them. It speaks about life and
love and joy and peace and rest.
If we get a house and put these into it,
we shall have a secured home.

John Henry Jowett

THE GUARDIAN ANGELS OF LIFE SOMETIMES
FLY SO HIGH AS TO BE BEYOND OUR SIGHT,
BUT THEY ARE ALWAYS LOOKING DOWN UPON US.

JEAN PAUL RICHTER

*God gives us always strength enough,
and sense enough, for everything
He wants us to do.*

JOHN RUSKIN

IT'S THE LITTLE THINGS THAT MAKE UP THE
RICHEST PART OF THE TAPESTRY OF OUR LIVES.

UNKNOWN

"Where your treasure is,
there your heart will be also."

MATTHEW 6:21 NIV

REJECTING THINGS BECAUSE THEY ARE
OLD-FASHIONED WOULD RULE OUT THE SUN
AND THE MOON, AND A MOTHER'S LOVE.

UNKNOWN

AND THROUGH THE YEARS, A MOTHER
HAS BEEN ALL THAT'S SWEET AND GOOD,
FOR THERE'S A BIT OF GOD AND LOVE
IN ALL TRUE MOTHERHOOD.

HELEN STEINER RICE

WEARE SO PRECIOUSLY LOVED BY GOD
THAT WE CANNOT EVEN COMPREHEND IT.
NO CREATED BEING CAN EVER KNOW
HOW MUCH AND HOW SWEETLY
AND TENDERLY GOD LOVES THEM.

JULIAN OF NORWICH

*Where can one better be than the bosom of one's own family?*

FRENCH PROVERB

TRAIN YOUR CHILD IN THE WAY IN WHICH
YOU KNOW YOU SHOULD HAVE GONE YOURSELF.

CHARLES H. SPURGEON

LET US BE GRATEFUL TO PEOPLE WHO
MAKE US HAPPY—THEY ARE THE CHARMING
GARDENERS WHO MAKE OUR SOULS BLOSSOM.

MARCEL PROUST

*A kindhearted woman gains respect.*

PROVERBS 11:16 NIV

*Love children especially. . . .*
*They live to soften and purify our hearts.*

FYODOR DOSTOEVSKY

THE FAMILY WAS FIRST ORDAINED BY
GOD THAT CHILDREN MIGHT BE TRAINED
UP FOR HIMSELF; IT WAS THE FIRST
FORM OF THE CHURCH ON EARTH.

POPE LEO XIII

*Where there is room in the heart,*
*there is always room in the house.*

THOMAS MORE

WHERE THE SOUL IS FULL OF PEACE
AND JOY, OUTWARD SURROUNDINGS
AND CIRCUMSTANCES ARE OF
COMPARATIVELY LITTLE ACCOUNT.

HANNAH WHITALL SMITH

When we start to count flowers,
we cease to count weeds;
When we start to count blessings,
we cease to count needs;
When we start to count laughter,
we cease to count tears;
When we start to count memories,
we cease to count years.

Unknown

GOD PROVIDES RESTING PLACES AS
WELL AS WORKING PLACES. REST, THEN,
AND BE THANKFUL WHEN HE BRINGS YOU,
WEARIED, TO A WAYSIDE WELL.

L. B. COWMAN

GOD SENDS US CHILDREN. . .TO ENLARGE OUR
HEARTS, TO MAKE US UNSELFISH AND FULL
OF KINDLY SYMPATHIES AND AFFECTIONS,
TO GIVE OUR SOULS HIGHER AIMS, TO CALL
OUT ALL OUR FACULTIES TO EXTENDED
ENTERPRISE AND EXERTION; TO BRING ROUND
OUR FIRESIDE BRIGHT FACES AND HAPPY
SMILES, AND LOVING, TENDER HEARTS.

MARY HOWITT

*He blesses the home of the righteous.*

PROVERBS 3:33 NIV

*Whoever walks toward God one step,*
*God runs toward him two.*

JEWISH PROVERB

WE WERE NOT SENT INTO THIS WORLD
TO DO ANYTHING INTO WHICH
WE CANNOT PUT OUR HEARTS.

JOHN RUSKIN

*Happiness is the atmosphere in which all good affections grow.*

ANNA ELIZA BRAY

A MOTHER IS NOT A PERSON TO LEAN ON,
BUT A PERSON TO MAKE LEANING UNNECESSARY.

DOROTHY CANFIELD FISHER

*A family holds hands
and sticks together.*

UNKNOWN

THAT ENERGY WHICH MAKES A CHILD
HARD TO MANAGE IS THE ENERGY WHICH
AFTERWARD MAKES HIM A MANAGER OF LIFE.

HENRY WARD BEECHER

*A small house will hold
as much happiness as a big one.*

Unknown

In order to manage children well,
we must borrow their eyes and their
hearts, see and feel as they do, and
judge them from their own point of view.

Eugénie de Guérin

*To understand your parents' love,
you must raise children yourself.*

CHINESE PROVERB

LOVE EACH OTHER WITH GENUINE AFFECTION,
AND TAKE DELIGHT IN HONORING EACH OTHER.

ROMANS 12:10 NLT

When I approach a child, he inspires in me two sentiments: tenderness for what he is, and respect for what he may become.

Louis Pasteur

IT IS LOVE THAT ASKS, THAT SEEKS,
THAT KNOCKS, THAT FINDS, AND THAT
IS FAITHFUL TO WHAT IT FINDS.

ST. AUGUSTINE

No joy is so sublimely affecting
as the joy of a mother at the
good fortune of her child.

JEAN PAUL RICHTER

WE FIND DELIGHT IN THE BEAUTY
AND HAPPINESS OF CHILDREN THAT MAKES
THE HEART TOO BIG FOR THE BODY.

RALPH WALDO EMERSON

*A family is a little world
created by love.*

UNKNOWN

A MOTHER'S LOVE LIVES ON. . . .
SHE REMEMBERS. . .HER CHILD'S MERRY
LAUGH, THE JOYFUL SHOUT OF HIS CHILDHOOD,
THE OPENING PROMISE OF HIS YOUTH.

WASHINGTON IRVING

*All thy children shall be taught of the Lord; and great shall be the peace of thy children.*

ISAIAH 54:13 KJV

CHILDREN MAKE LOVE STRONGER,
DAYS SHORTER, NIGHTS LONGER,
BANKROLLS SMALLER, HOMES HAPPIER,
CLOTHES SHABBIER, THE PAST FORGOTTEN,
AND THE FUTURE WORTH LIVING FOR.

UNKNOWN

*Children are poor people's riches.*

English Proverb

ALLOW CHILDREN TO BE HAPPY IN
THEIR OWN WAY, FOR WHAT BETTER
WAY WILL THEY EVER FIND?

SAMUEL JOHNSON

HOME IS THE ONE PLACE IN ALL THIS WORLD
WHERE HEARTS ARE SURE OF EACH OTHER.

FREDERICK W. ROBERTSON

TO A CHILD, LOVE IS SPELLED T-I-M-E.

UNKNOWN

*A mother's love endures through all.*

WASHINGTON IRVING

God knows everything about us.
And He cares about everything.
Moreover, He can manage every situation.
And He loves us!

Hannah Whitall Smith

*Every good and perfect
gift is from above.*

JAMES 1:17 NIV

You can do anything with children
if you only play with them.

Otto von Bismarck

*Give a little love to a child
and you get a great deal back.*

JOHN RUSKIN

HAPPY WILL THAT HOUSE BE IN WHICH
RELATIONS ARE FORMED FROM CHARACTER.

RALPH WALDO EMERSON

Sometimes I wonder–what kind of
example am I leaving my children?
What will they write on my tombstone
or say about me after I'm gone? . . .
Hopefully my epitaph will read something
like this: "She hated folding laundry
but liked to fold us in her arms."

Dena Dyer

*No one is useless in this world who lightens the burdens of it for another.*

CHARLES DICKENS

*God has something new for you every day. He delights in you and loves to surprise you with good things.*

UNKNOWN

THERE IS NOTHING HIGHER AND STRONGER
AND MORE WHOLESOME AND USEFUL FOR
LIFE IN LATER YEARS THAN SOME GOOD MEMORY,
ESPECIALLY A MEMORY CONNECTED WITH
CHILDHOOD, WITH HOME.

FYODOR DOSTOEVSKY

No one is a failure who has
helped hold happily a home together.
Those who have been victorious in their
homes can never be completely defeated.

Robert Burns

*The riches that are in
the heart cannot be stolen.*

RUSSIAN PROVERB

*Let the peace of Christ
rule in your hearts.*

COLOSSIANS 3:15 NIV

IF YOU WOULD HAVE YOUR CHILDREN TO
WALK HONORABLY THROUGH THE WORLD,
YOU MUST NOT ATTEMPT TO CLEAR THE
STONES FROM THEIR PATH, BUT TEACH THEM
TO WALK FIRMLY OVER THEM—NOT INSIST
UPON LEADING THEM BY THE HAND,
BUT LET THEM LEARN TO GO ALONE.

ANNE BRONTË

TIME HAS A WAY OF SHOWING US
WHAT REALLY MATTERS.

UNKNOWN

*Children have more need
of models than of critics.*

JOSEPH JOUBERT

THERE IS A RELIGION IN ALL DEEP LOVE,
BUT THE LOVE OF A MOTHER IS THE
VEIL OF A SOFTER LIGHT BETWEEN THE
HEART AND THE HEAVENLY FATHER.

SAMUEL TAYLOR COLERIDGE

When God thought of mother,
He must have laughed with satisfaction,
and framed it quickly—so rich, so deep,
so divine, so full of soul, power,
and beauty was the conception!

Henry Ward Beecher

TO BE A CHILD IS TO KNOW THE JOY OF LIVING.
TO HAVE A CHILD IS TO KNOW THE BEAUTY OF LIFE.

UNKNOWN

*Praise the children
and they will blossom.*

IRISH PROVERB

"I WILL POUR OUT MY SPIRIT ON YOUR OFFSPRING,
AND MY BLESSING ON YOUR DESCENDANTS."

ISAIAH 44:3 NIV

WE CAN'T FORM OUR CHILDREN ON
OUR OWN CONCEPTS; WE MUST TAKE THEM
AND LOVE THEM AS GOD GIVES THEM TO US.

JOHANN WOLFGANG VON GOETHE

to close the studio and just leave town. It's not safe
for me anymore."

"Don't be ridiculous," Jasper replies. "You will
do what I tell you to do."

"So Jean and Jasper are working together," I say
when it comes to an end. "Maybe she's hiding something for him? Maybe it was him calling Dad from
her phone."

"Maybe." Crow nods slowly. I know he wants to
say something, but he's hesitating.

"What?" I ask.

He touches the stubble on his jawline. "I'm surprised you haven't come up with the most obvious
conclusion, which is that your dad and Jean had something to do with each other."

My mouth opens and closes again. "My dad never
dated anyone after my mom. He said he never would,
because there was no one else for him except her."

I realize how ridiculous it sounds when I say it
out loud. I grew up hearing this, and believing it.
Then I think of that scarf. Maybe what Crow is
saying is true. It's still a hard pill for me to swallow. I
told my dad I'd be happy for him if he moved
on, and he assured me he was fine as he was. I even
asked if he was dating and he said no.

"At the end of the day, he was still a man," he says
rubbing my knuckles with his fingers. "And
honestly, babe. Imagine being alone all of
these years. All I'm saying is, you never know. With
whatever they spoke on the phone, and for

## Chapter Sixteen

"You look familiar," one of the customers says to
Cam, who is having none of it.

"I used to do porn, so maybe that's why," she replies, flashing him a sarcastic smile and walking
away.

I try to stop myself from laughing, but I can't.
Still, I pull myself together as the man approaches me
with some merchandise in his hands. "I'm guessing
that's a no, she doesn't want to give me her number,"
he grumbles, placing the helmet and jacket down on
the desk.

"You should try some new lines," I suggest, smiling. "But she *is* seeing someone, so they probably
wouldn't have worked anyway."

"Noted," he replies, nodding. "How about you?
Are you single?"

I blink slowly at the man, any sympathy I have for
him being rejected by Cam disappearing. Do men really think women would take them up on an offer of
being second place? Surely not.

"No, I'm not," I reply, placing his items in a bag. "That will be three hundred and seventy dollars."

He pays in cash and leaves without saying anything further, which I appreciate. Cam comes back out, laughing when I tell her what happened.

"Men are something else." She smirks, shaking her head. "Lucky Crow isn't here or he'd be leaving without a limb."

"And if Billie was here?" I tease.

"Probably without one of his nuts."

"So you two are all good then?" I pry, sitting back in my seat and wiggling my brows. "Exclusive, even?"

"Well, we haven't put a label on it," she admits, not seeming bothered by that fact. "I don't know. We're just having some fun. I'm just going to take it as it comes. Ha, as it comes."

"You're the worst," I deadpan, just as Nadia steps into the warehouse and beelines for me.

"Hey, Bronte."

"Nadia. What's up? Is everything okay?" I ask, standing.

"Everything is fine, I just have some information for you," she states, handing me a folder. "I typed out some of the conversations I overheard from Jean for you. I think you might find them interesting."

Eyes widening, I pull out the first piece of paper, and read.

"It's Freddy's daughter, Jasper, she knows something. I don't know what to do, I think I

should leave town. Why else would she come to my studio? She knows."

"That snake," I murmur to myself. "Jasper. Where have I heard that name before?"

"He was on the list," Nadia says, crossing her arms over her chest. "He's one of the men trying to take over Grayson's territory."

"Who the hell is Grayson?"

"Your uncle Neville," she explains, telling me how apparently he goes by different names. Nothing my uncle does at this point is going to surprise me.

"So Jean has ties to Dad and to one of the suspect list. What do you do now?" I ing. "Tell me what *I* need to do."

"I think we should wait and se says," she says, looking down at th more proof and we need to kn before we go in guns blazin

But it's not looking go dad, or was it Jasper? C

I read the rest of t give anything els is connected to what she wa

But I w

When Cro to the new re tening to her vol

*"They are onto u*

the length of their conversations, it's leaning toward them having some kind of relationship."

"He wasn't alone all of those years—he had me," I say, even though I know exactly what he meant. Swallowing hard, I listen to reason. "Okay, maybe you're right. But maybe you're not."

"Just keep an open mind," he says, kissing my temple. "That's all I'm asking. And you know what? If he did have something with her, he didn't do anything wrong."

"Why didn't he tell me? If this woman hypothetically did mean something to him, why did he keep it a secret?"

Why couldn't he come to me with this, and be honest about his own life?

"Maybe because you'd take it really hard, like you are right now at just the possibility?" he suggests.

Fuck.

"My mom was the love of his life—"

"And I'm sure she still was, but that doesn't mean you can't enjoy the company of someone else. Especially when your mom had been gone for so long. There are different kinds of love. Not all are the soul-connecting kind. Just being simply happy with someone's company isn't a crime."

Gritting my teeth together, I nod slowly. "Okay, you're right."

That doesn't mean it doesn't hurt any less, though. I know I'm holding my dad to an impossible standard, but he's the one who set that standard, so I don't understand how I'm supposed to react right now.

*If* this is the truth.

"Do you think it was Jasper who did something to Dad?" I ask, resting my head on Crow's shoulder and staring straight ahead at the TV. "Maybe he was jealous over Jean, or maybe he just wanted him gone so he could take over."

"I think we'll find out in the next few days," he says, kissing the top of my head. "And then we will make a plan. But either way, they aren't going to get away with what they've done. They've messed with the wrong family."

He's not wrong.

Nothing can bring Dad back now, but at least I can make sure he gets justice.

Before bed, I give Nadia a quick call and update her on everything I found out.

"Bronte, it's getting dangerous now. I'll keep listening in, but we need to leave the rest of it up to the MC and your uncle," she states. "Be careful. This Jasper guy is no joke, and we need to protect ourselves."

"I know," I reply.

But we're close.

I can feel it.


"Where's Crow?" I ask Chains as he steps into Fast & Fury. He's wearing all black, his dark eyes alert, hair slicked back. He's such a wildcard, and I never know how to act around him. He's intimidating.

"He can't come in today, so I'm covering for him," he says, coming over, eyes pinned on me. "He said he will come to your place later tonight."

"Okay," I reply, sitting down at my desk. "Let me know if there's anything I can do to help you today."

"I'm good," he grits out, face expressionless. "But thanks."

He walks off to the garage and disappears inside. Cam comes over and sits down on my desk as she looks over some documents. "This next bike is going to be insane. You should see the design for the spray paint." She beams, showing me her idea.

"I love that," I tell her, checking out the black, white and red design. "Who is it for?"

"Some rich guy." She shrugs, pushing her blond hair out of her eyes. "He said to do whatever, no cost is too high, and he wants the best of the best for everything."

"Imagine what that must be like." I grin, looking back at my screen. Meanwhile, I have a thousand dollars in my account and that's it. I haven't reached out to my dad's lawyer about his will and money, even though he sent me an email trying to set up an appointment. I know I'm going to have to deal with the house and all the money and everything, but I'm just not ready yet. I want to find out who killed him before a single cent leaves his account.

"Must be nice," Cam agrees, placing the design down on the table and looking towards the garage. "I better get some work done."

"Me too."

Abbie comes in for lunch, and it's nice to see her face.

"How are you?" I ask, giving her a tight hug.

"I'm good. I brought us all lunch," she says, placing Chinese food down on the table. "I feel like I haven't seen you all in ages; I've been so busy with exams. Crow has been keeping me up to date on everything, but how are you feeling? If you need anything you know I'm just a call away, right?"

"I know," I reply. "To be honest, I've just been keeping busy with this whole thing, and it's distracting me. And Crow has been amazing. I don't know how I would have gotten through this without him."

"He is, isn't he?" She smiles, opening the food and spreading it all out. "You two are going to get married and have lots of kids. I can see it now."

I look down so she can't see my expression at the mention of kids. "I don't know about all that, but I'm pretty damn lucky that I met him. Which I suppose I owe to you."

"You don't owe me anything. I'm just glad you're in our lives, Bronte," she says as she gives me another hug. "Seriously, I didn't realize anything was missing in my life until I met you. I can't wait for you to meet my sister when she comes down next. She's going to love you."

"I'd like that," I reply, beaming at her kind words. "And you guys are my family now, so I'm grateful for each and every one of you." I lower my voice and add, "Even Chains."

Abbie laughs out loud. "He'll grow on you. Slowly. Kind of like a fungus. He's hard to get to know and guarded as hell, but once he knows you're here to stay, he'll accept you. And he will be there for you."

I decide to ask Abbie something that has been on my mind for a while now.

"So…are you basically the queen of the MC?" I ask her. "Temper is the president, so that makes you on the top of the food chain, right?"

Abbie looks surprised at first, and then starts laughing. "I mean, I've never really thought about it like that, but yes, I'm the president's old lady and everyone shows me respect. I give that respect right back, though, so there's never been any kind of issue. I don't feel any different than the other women. We're all friends, so yeah."

I blink slowly. "So…you're the queen."

She laughs some more.

"What else do I need to know about MC life?" I ask.

"Well, the men all have their own positions in the club. Their tasks and responsibilities, all of which could change at any point, are given to them," she explains, giving me the rundown. "They have to listen to Temper, as he's their leader. And whatever he says goes. They have private meetings and they do all kind of biker things, like club runs, charity events, which I sometimes host, and whatever other personal business they attend to."

Sounds like a pretty good life, being Temper, but I guess when something goes wrong that's all on him, too.

"So it's basically like…a totalitarian, illegal country club?" I ask, trying to understand it all.

She laughs even harder.

"What?" I ask, her laugh making me laugh too.

Chains walks over and eyes her. "You've broken her," he says to me.

Once she's calmed down, we all sit together and eat. Like a Fast & Fury family.

# Chapter Seventeen

When Crow knocks at my apartment door I meet him in a black teddy, stiletto heels, and nothing else.

"Wow" is the first word he says, taking me in from head to toe. "Fucking hell, Bronte, you trying to kill me or what?"

Grinning and loving his reaction, I pull him inside and close the door behind him, pushing him back against it. "I missed you."

"So did I," he grits out, running his hands over the lace covering my breasts. "You are so sexy, you have no idea. I've been thinking about you and all the things I want to do with you all day…"

"And now you get to have me," I reply, kissing him and all but climbing up his body like a tree. Holding me up with his strong hands on my ass cheeks, massaging the globes, he carries me to the couch, never removing his lips from mine, and lays me back. He smells so good, and I can't wait to have him inside of me.

I've been waiting for this all day.

I've never known what it's like to crave someone

like this—I feel like with my exes I could give or take being with them, but it's nothing like that with Crow.

I want him. All of him.

His company, his time, his body, his laugh. His mind.

I can't get enough.

I can feel how hard he is, his cock pressed against me, and I can't help but touch him with my hand, stroking him over the material of his jeans. I love how I drive him crazy, and the feeling is mutual.

He makes a growling noise and grabs my hands, pinning them both above my head, kissing my neck while grinding himself on me. After letting go of me, he rips apart the bodysuit part of my teddy, exposing me to his lips. I loved that teddy, but I don't care, because that was so hot and so worth it. Gripping his hair, I arch my hips and moan as he licks my pussy and then slides his tongue up to my clit, sucking on it.

I know I'm not going to last long, especially if he keeps working on me like that.

"Crow," I moan, trying to make this last a little longer, because it feels so damn good, but his tongue works his magic and has me coming loudly, my thighs trembling so hard.

Crow flips me over, bending me over the couch, then removes his jeans and briefs and slides inside me in one smooth thrust.

"Fuck," he whispers, gripping my hips and moving back and forth. He leans over me and kisses my neck, then puts his hand underneath me to gently stroke my already sensitive clit.

"I love you," he says into my ear. "So much."

I can't seem to form a reply as he keeps stroking me until I come again, this time with him.

"I love you too," I say as I roll over and he pulls me into his arms.

He grins, and I fall in love with him all over again.

"You rode on the bike today?" Cam asks as I step into the warehouse.

"What gives that away?" I ask, laughing as I touch my hair, which is all messy. "Oh, that would do it."

"Man, I love Crow's bike. It's so sexy," she says, perving on it from the entrance of the garage. Crow is doing the same thing, which is why he hasn't come inside yet.

"Have you ridden on it?" I ask casually, combing my hair with my fingers.

She gives me an odd look. "No. The men don't let just anyone on their bikes."

"What do you mean?" I ask, frowning. "Not even a friend?"

She shrugs and keeps staring at the bike. "Maybe a friend if it was necessary, but no, usually just their women. Their old ladies. No one else."

I had no idea this was even a thing, but I guess it makes sense. They take their bikes very seriously. "Interesting," I reply, retying my hair in a tight ponytail. "That's kind of nice. Not that I'd care if you or any of my friends went for a ride with him, though, for the record."

"Noted." She grins, sighing when the phone starts

to ring. "Today is going to be insane. We have three custom bikes being picked up, and we have a few clients coming in to tell us what they want when it comes time for us to do their bikes."

"I'm on it," I say, heading to answer the phone.

Crow comes in just as I hang up from a customer. "Nadia just called me," he says, palms on my desk. "You weren't answering your phone. She said she wants to speak to us."

"Now?"

He nods.

"I can't leave now, today is busy," I explain, brows drawing together. "How about after work? We can't just leave everyone high and dry." Although I'm dying to know what new information Nadia has, we can't leave Cam alone.

"You need to hire more people," I also suggest. "I know it's a small business, but it's also very busy and we could always use an extra set of hands."

He grins and nods. "Okay, and yeah, I agree. We're looking for more mechanics right now."

"Good," I say, blowing him a kiss and then getting back to work.

The day goes quickly, and Cam was right, it *is* insane. I end up eating at my desk and still answering phones, unable to leave for even a few minutes. When we close up, Crow and I ride back to the clubhouse. We told Nadia to meet us there. She beats us, and we find her out the back with Dee, while Saint and Skylar are in the kitchen cooking dinner together.

"Hey," I say as I sit down next to them. "Sorry we couldn't leave the garage earlier."

"No problem," she replies, picking up her phone and hitting play. "Just thought the two of you would want to hear this."

*"Why do you keep talking about his daughter? Who cares, she has no proof. His death isn't being treated as suspicious, and we have nothing to worry about. What, are you missing your lover? Maybe you're having regrets? Why else do you keep bringing this bitch up?"*

*"Maybe because I don't want to go to prison,"* Jean fires back. *"And I didn't kill him, Jasper. You did."*

*"You didn't stop me,"* Jasper replies. *"You knew the plan, and you went along with it. You're in this as much as I am. And we need to stick together. We're almost at the top—there's no time for panic to creep in. We just need to take out Grayson, and we've won. We'll be on top of the fucking city."*

Nadia hits stop and looks over at us. "Now we know the truth. The question is, what do you want to do about it?"

I don't reply, because I'm still processing what I've just heard. Crow was right—Dad did have some kind of relationship with Jean, one he kept hidden from everyone, and she was a weakness that cost him his life. I can't believe this. He was finally opening up to a woman, and in the end she screwed him over.

I don't know who this Jasper is, but he's not going to harm my uncle.

And he's not going to be on top of fucking any-thing, not if I have anything to do about it.

"You okay?" Crow asks, touching my shoulder.

I don't know what the two of them have been say-ing this entire time. I've blocked it out, too in my head.

"I will be," I reply, exhaling deeply. "What do you think we should do? I want to take him down. I want to make sure he can't hurt my uncle, or anyone for that matter."

"I think we should talk to your uncle," Crow says, and Nadia nods. "He needs to know what's going on, and who is coming for him." Crow turns to me, opens his mouth, and then closes it, seemingly try-ing to choose his words carefully. "You need to let us handle this now, okay? And you need to not ask questions that you don't want the answers to. Think about what you can and can't handle, Bronte."

"Nadia?" I press.

"Why don't we just call the police and get them involved?" she says.

"What are they going to do?" Crow replies, brow furrowing. "You're going to leave this in the hands of the people who wouldn't even press for a further investigation? As far as they're concerned, Freddy died from an overdose. We'll probably be the ones that end up getting arrested."

I know what Crow is saying, and he's right. I can't trust the cops to sort this out, not the way I want it handled. Now it's out of my hands and I need to leave it up to the MC and my uncle.

Jasper might end up in a ditch somewhere, and I need to be okay with that. I can't come this far, say that I want him gone, but then be a bleeding heart and feel bad about it.

And if I can't handle it, then I need to step back and not ask any questions.

"I know what you're saying. It's just hard because this is my fight. I can't expect anyone else to—"

"You are both nice girls," Dee says, cutting me off. "You don't need to go down this route. We can handle it along with your uncle, okay? We're not good men, Bronte. And neither is your uncle. We're all good to you, and we always will be good to you, but that doesn't make us good men. In this case, we're the only ones who are going to be able to give you the revenge you want."

I don't know what to say. I know they are right, but it doesn't feel good leaving everyone else to fight my fight.

Nadia heads home after I thank her for her help. I know she doesn't like the way it ended, but I need to go with my gut. And the cops aren't the answer this time.

"Can we go to my uncle's now?"

Crow nods. "Sure. Do you want to give him a call and make sure he's home?"

I call him up and ask him where he is.

"I'm at home, why? Is everything okay?"

"Yeah, I was just wondering if Crow and I could drop in? I wanted to talk to you about a few things."

And to play him that recording Nadia sent us so he can hear it for himself.

"Of course," he says quickly. "I'll be waiting for you."

"Okay, see you soon." We hang up and I look to Crow. "Let's go."

Standing, I give Dee a hug. "Thank you for all that you do. To me, you're not a bad man. Just an honest one."

And I mean that.

I guess he's right, though—when you decide if someone is a good person, you judge them by how they treat you, not others. Our perception of people is only as we see them, not as they are.

We get in the car and head to see my uncle.

It's time that the truth got out.

# Chapter Eighteen

Uncle Neville's waiting out front by the gate when we arrive, two bodyguards behind him. He presses a code and signals us to drive in. We park behind his black Mercedes and hop out.

"Is everything okay?" he says as he gives me a hug. He looks worried, lips tight and brow tense. "Tell me what's going on."

"Can we go inside first?" I suggest.

"Of course."

He leads us inside his beautiful mansion, and to the living room. He offers us refreshments, which we decline, wanting to get straight to business. Crow pulls out his phone, his finger lingering on the play button.

"We have something we want to you listen to," I say, taking Uncle Neville's hand in mine and giving it a squeeze. This is going to be hard for him to listen to, too. "We found out what happened to Dad."

We press play, and I watch the myriad emotions flicker in his eyes.

Pain.

Anger.

Regret.

Disbelief.

"That fucking piece of shit," he growls, stands up and starts pacing. The vein in his forehead looks like it's going to burst. His anger justifies my own——he feels the same way that I do.

"You know him personally, then?" Crow guesses, sliding his phone back in his jean pocket. "What are we up against here?"

"I've done business with Jasper," he admits, hands clenching to fists. He then brings his eyes to me. "And I've met Jean. Once."

"So she and Dad were together?" I ask, swallowing hard.

And once again I was the last to know something. I wish people would just be honest and let me decide what I can and can't handle.

"He introduced her as a friend," he explains, sitting back down, scrubbing his hand down his face. "I think there was something more going on, yes. I'm so sorry, Bronte. This all must be so hard for you."

It is, but I need to know all of it. "I wanted the truth, and I got it. I just need to know what's going to happen now," I say, looking him in the eye. "They're going to come after you next. What are we going to do?"

"If he could get to me, he would have already," he says, tapping his foot on the tiles. "I upped my security, and this place was already secure to begin with. I have cameras everywhere, so even if something happened, it would be seen. His only chance would be to get to me when I'm out somewhere, but I have my security with me, and he's clearly a coward, going by the way Freddy died. There was no fight. He simply poisoned him using Jean, I'm assuming. You don't have to worry about me. He's the one who needs to worry. Now that I know the truth, I'm going to fuck shit up."

The look he has in his eyes, I've never seen it before. He's furious, and out for revenge.

"What can I do to help?" I ask.

"Stay safe." He turns to Crow. "Keep her safe. They know that she knows something. Tell me if you want some of my men to watch her. Whatever you need, I've got."

"She's safe with me," Crow replies, lifting his chin. "Always will be."

"I know." Neville nods, respect in his eyes. "Thank you for finding out the truth, Bronte. You're a strong girl, you know that? And you were the apple of your father's eye. He loved you more than he loved anything or anyone in the world."

And the feeling was reciprocated.

"I know," I whisper, forcing a smile and giving him a hug. "I love you."

"I love you too," he says, squeezing me tightly. We stay like that for a few moments, and then I leave, feeling emotional but happy that the conversation transpired.

Billie calls me on the way home. "Hey, what are you up to?" she asks.

I expel a deep sigh. "Just left my uncle's house. What's going on with you?"

"Nothing much," she admits. "I just miss you, so I thought I'd call and annoy you a little bit. Did you still want me to stop by your dad's place and get the box the movers forgot?"

"Yes, please, if you don't mind. That would be awesome," I say. I asked her to do it since it's still hard for me to go there.

"When am I seeing you next?"

"I'll drop in tomorrow night."

"Sounds perfect. See you then. Love you."

"Love you, too."

We hang up. Crow and I head back to the club-house, and all I can think is, what the hell is going to happen next?

A beautiful blonde walks into the warehouse, black heels clicking with each step. Her white bodysuit tucked into denim shorts show off her stunning fig-ure, and her light eyes scan the room.

"Hey," she says, smiling at me. "Is Crow here?"

"Ummm, yes, he is," I reply, eyes slightly narrow-ing. "One second."

Disappearing out the back, I approach Crow, who is kneeling near a motorcycle, examining it. "Crow, there's a gorgeous blonde at the front desk asking for you."

He lifts his head, brows drawing together. "What?"

"Yep," I reply, trying to keep my expression neutral. I have no idea who she is or what she wants, but after reading a romance novel last night, I picture the same thing that happened to the heroine happening to me. Now this woman is here to tell Crow she's pregnant from before he met me, and he's going to be a dad.

Just what I need right now.

Wincing, I walk beside him back to her. It better not be the case, because I'm not dealing with any baby mamas.

"Crow!" the woman yells out, smiling widely as she runs to him and throws herself in his arms. "I'm home. And I need the spare house keys. I accidentally left mine in my room."

"Heidi," he murmurs, smiling. He puts her down and pulls me next to him. "That definitely sounds like you. This is Bronte. Bronte, this is my baby sister."

"Oh," I mutter, eyes widening. Of course it's his sister. Blonde. Attractive. Why the hell didn't I think of that? This is the second time I've assumed something out of nothing and looked like an asshole. I don't miss Crow's smirk as he introduces us. I should be glad that it's not an ex or baby mama, yet I still feel a little on the embarrassed side.

Good one, Bronte.

I need to control my jealousy around this man, because it's really not that cute.

"Nice to finally meet you, Heidi."

"You too," she replies, glancing between the two of us. "My brother can't stop talking about you, and I can see why—you're absolutely gorgeous. I'd expect nothing else from Crow."

"I was thinking the same about you," I reply, smiling.

Crow fishes a set of keys out of his pocket and removes one. "Here you go."

"Thanks," she replies, sliding the keys into her own pocket. "What are you both doing tonight? Do you want to come over for dinner?"

Crow looks down at me, and I nod. "Sure, why not?"

"Perfect. I'll see you both around seven?"

"Sounds good," Crow replies. I ignore his gaze while Heidi clicks away.

"You thought it was an ex-girlfriend or something, didn't you?" He laughs, lifting me up and setting me down on my desk. "You should have seen your face."

"She's young and beautiful," I reply, raising my chin and shrugging. "And she was asking for you. It's a valid conclusion."

"Even if someone came here looking for me, it doesn't matter. I choose you over anyone, past, present or future, all right? You're it for me, and my eyes sure as hell aren't wandering," he assures me, kissing my cheek. "Although you look cute when you're mad."

He laughs as he walks away.

Jerk.

Still, his words are comforting to hear. He's a good-looking man, and I know he'll have women wanting him always. But he's mine.

And I'm not going to share.

Nadia comes into the garage, which is a first, but the second I see the look on her face, I know that something is very wrong. Her eyes are red like she's been crying, and her arms are wrapped around herself.

"What is it?" I ask, getting up and going to her. I place my hands on her shoulders. "Nadia? What's happened?"

"It's Billie," she explains. "I'm so sorry, Bronte."

"Billie? What about Billie?" I ask, my heart in my throat. "I just spoke to her yesterday, and she's fine."

"She's gone," Nadia whispers, swallowing hard. "I heard it over the police radio, and then I called my contacts to be certain and…" She takes a deep breath. "She was shot at your dad's house. His address is what drew my attention first."

"What?" I whisper, shaking my head.

"Police responded to shots fired at your dad's address and they found her in front of the house. Do you know why she was…" Nadia can't seem to continue as I start to fall apart.

"It was because of me. I was such a baby and didn't want to go back to my dad's house to pick up the last box there. So I asked her to go for me. Why did I ask her? Why couldn't I just do something on my own for once? Why…"

Nadia pulls me in for a hug. "Shhh, stop that right there."

I just lost my dad, and now Billie, the girl who's like a sister to me.

This can't be happening.

I sit down on my chair and cover my face with my

hands, just straight out sobbing. How much more of this am I supposed to take before I break?

Cam comes out of the staff room and rushes over to me. "Why are you crying, Bronte? What's wrong?"

I'm crying too hard, I can't even reply, so Nadia informs her.

And then I have to watch Cam's heart break in front of my eyes.

She shakes her head in disbelief. "No, she can't be gone."

She takes one look at my face, and starts crying with me, holding me. I don't know who is comforting who, but we both need it.

"This is all my fault," I say to them both.

"The only person at fault is whoever shot her," Nadia replies, wiping tears away from my face. "And I know who my bet is on."

Nadia obviously assumes it has something to do with our case, and if that's true then it's my fault Billie is gone right now. Why would someone want to harm her? It makes no sense.

What the fuck have I done, getting her involved in all of this?


"I'm not going to let them hurt anyone else that I love!" I yell at Crow in the car. We cancel on dinner with Heidi and tell her we will make it up to her. When she hears what has happened, she understands instantly and sends her condolences.

I know I shouldn't take my pain out on Crow, but he's the only one here and he's the closest person to me in the world. I never thought a man other than my dad would ever be that for me.

"I know," he says gently, reaching over and taking my hand. "But this isn't your fault."

"I should have just stayed away from her until this was over," I whisper to myself, my hands clenching to fists. "I can't believe this has happened."

It all feels unreal, like a dream. Or maybe I haven't processed it properly yet. I feel numb, just when I was starting to feel again. I feel so damn guilty that it's eating me inside. Billie was a good person, and she didn't deserve this.

"It's not your fault," Crow repeats, pulling into the police station. We're going to speak to them about Billie, to get any extra information they might have for us. We're also meeting my dad's lawyer here, because I know that they are going to want to question me.

Crow can tell me it's not my fault all he likes. He can scream it at me until he's blue in the face. It wouldn't make a difference.

I brought her into this.

If it weren't for me, she'd still be alive and happy, maybe in love with Cam.

Another innocent life, lost.

And I'm the thing they all have in common.

## Chapter Nineteen

I take the rest of the week off work. After talking to the police, they let me know that I'm not a suspect and I don't have to go back to the station. Crow hires two new people, so I don't feel so guilty about sitting around in my underwear for a few days. Crow, Saint, Renny and Temper come to my apartment to install security cameras and put extra locks on all the doors and windows. Better to be safe than sorry, they say.

But it's too late for Billie, and right now I don't really care what happens to me. I just want everyone else to be safe.

Am I supposed to just hang around until my uncle sorts this out? Is he going to kill Jasper? What's going to happen to Jean? I wish I knew what his plan was. I'd rather the two of them end up in prison than be killed, if I'm being honest, but I know it's up to them to handle the situation as they see fit.

"Hey," Crow says as he steps inside, locking the door behind him. "Have you moved from that spot since I left this morning?"

"Yes, I went to the fridge and the bathroom," I

reply, smiling at him sadly. "How was work? How are the new staff?"

Small talk. Small talk is safe, and I'd rather talk about anything other than how I feel right now.

"They're good. I should have hired people sooner," he admits, sitting down close to me. "Everyone is worried about you, and asking when you'll be back."

"I'm the worst employee ever," I say, sighing and resting my cheek on his shoulder. "Lucky I have a good boss, huh?" Any other job and I'd definitely be fired by now.

"Your job is always there for you," he promises, pressing his lips against my temple. "And if you don't want it, and you need to take a break from work completely, that's okay too. You've been through more than any one person should, so no one would blame you if you need a break."

"I want to work," I tell him, frowning. I've never not worked, and I'm not someone who would ever be okay with not paying my own way. I wasn't raised like that. But I appreciate his offer and understand where he's coming from, wanting me to put my mental health first. Crow really is a man who looks after his woman, physically, mentally, emotionally...and even financially. Even though I wouldn't accept that, it hasn't gone unnoticed.

"Just saying, you do have options," he says gently. "I spoke to your uncle today."

"What did he say?" I ask.

"He said he has a plan and needs a little time, and

for us not to worry. Just try to stay safe, and he's handling it," Crow explains.

How am I supposed to not worry?

As much as I appreciate my uncle handling things, I want my say in what is going to happen. I don't like that decisions are being made without my involvement. Maybe Nadia was right and we should've gone to the police. At least then I'd be able to look my father's killer in the eye.

"Okay." I sigh. "I just want all of this to be over, you know? I'm glad we found out the truth about everything, but it came with a price."

A price too high: a life. Something I can't afford or replace.

Billie.

Closing my eyes, I picture her beautiful face, and wish that things were different. She was the sister I never had, the person who knew me better than anyone else besides my dad.

But I can't change what happened. And the only thing I can do now is see this through, and try not to let the guilt and regret eat me from the inside out.

"You can't look at it like that," Crow murmurs, standing up and pulling me with him. "Come on, let's make some dinner. You need to eat."

"Okay," I reply, following him into the kitchen. I go through the motions, but the truth is that with every tragedy I'm changing, evolving, and I don't know if that's a good or bad thing.

Grief is a monster.

We cook spaghetti together, and not for the first

time I thank my lucky stars that Crow came into my life. With all the bad going on, I don't want to ever forget the good, and he's really being my strength through everything that has happened.

"I love you," I say, stopping him in his tracks with my hand on his chest. "Like, I really, really love you."

Completely.

"I love you too," he replies, smiling widely, picking me up and placing me on the counter. "And we're always going to be okay. No matter what life throws at us, we're going to handle it. Together."

Together.

After the funeral, I go home and cry. No one should have to attend two funerals in the same month. It's just not fair, but I guess life never is. It's hard to look at the bright side, or to be grateful that I'm still here, but I need to. I know Dad would want me to live my life, and Billie would too.

"The speech you made was beautiful," Crow says as he sits down on my bed. "You're a good friend."

I feel like a virus that just keeps infecting people. "I don't feel like a good friend," I say into my pillow.

"Well, you are," he says, rubbing my back. "I know you're going through a really hard time right now, but you're going to be okay. You will get through this. Tomorrow is a new day, and so is the day after that. You won't have to relive this one."

The thought that I don't have to ever relive this day ever again is more comforting than I'd have known.

"I love you," I say, once again muffled by the material.

He laughs softly and kisses the back of my head. "I love you too. I'm going to cook some dinner, and then the prez wants to see me, so I have to pop into the clubhouse."

"Okay."

Once I'm alone, I think about everything that has happened. I can't just lie here waiting, hoping that this whole situation will go away. When is it going to be handled, and what does that even mean? What's going to happen to them? I need to know.

I need closure.

And I'm not going to be able to let go until I get it.

The words "I need to speak to you" have me looking up into the eyes of none other than Jean.

"You have some fucking nerve showing up here," I say, glancing around. Cam is in the garage, so if I call out to her she'll get here quickly.

Jean holds her hands up. "It's your safe space, so I thought you'd feel less threatened. I just want to have a chat and explain some things to you, and then I'll leave."

I eye her. I want to know what she has to say, but at the same time I know she doesn't deserve the time of day.

Curiosity wins out. "What do you want to talk about?"

"I loved your father," she admits, ducking her face. "I know you probably won't believe me, but I did."

I don't think she knows what love is. I don't want her to stop talking, though, so I cut off any harsh remarks and decide to press her further.

"How did you both meet?" I ask, hoping to finally get some answers.

"He came into my dance studio. He had a bucket list of things he wanted to try that he was going through, and a dance lesson was one of them," she explains.

I remember his bucket list. He was slowly ticking off a list of things he had never done, trying to experience more to life than just the daily grind. I remember him telling me some of the things he wanted to try.

Indoor skydiving.

To drive a racecar.

To run a marathon.

A cooking class.

I remember thinking it was cute, and that he was trying to live his best life.

"And then what?" I press.

"And then we became friends, and then it turned to more. We went on dates." She trails off, staring out the window. "He told me he had a daughter, one he loved very much and was proud of."

She looks at me. "I didn't hurt your father, and I want you to know that. I wouldn't do anything to him. He meant the world to me."

I can't contain my tongue any further.

"You poisoned him," I point out. "How is that not hurting him?"

"I didn't poison him," she vehemently denies.

"How do you know Jasper?" I ask, not believing a single word she said. I heard the conversation. Yes, she said it was Jasper that killed him, but she had involvement in it, too, and she can't pretend that she didn't.

I don't know how much she thinks I know, but I need to use this opportunity to get some answers.

"Jasper was my first husband," she admits, wrapping her arms around herself. "We've been divorced for several years now, and once I was out with Freddy and he saw us. And he recognized Freddy. He knew who he was, and he wanted something. And when Jasper wants something, he won't stop until he gets it. He said..." She pauses, a tear escaping her eyes. "He said if I didn't do as he wanted, he would hurt Anne, and I couldn't let them happen."

"Who is Anne?"

"Our daughter," she says, closing her eyes and taking a deep breath. "My daughter. Jasper isn't her father, but he met me when she was a baby, so he raised her."

I can't believe he'd threaten his own child, biological or not. If I ever adopted a child, I'd love that child just the same, and I'd never do anything to harm them. "If that doesn't show what kind of man he is..."

"I know," she huffs. "And I know he would do it. I know who he is. He's a violent man, that's why I finally left and divorced him after years of domestic abuse."

"So he told you to help him kill my dad or he was

going to hurt your daughter?" I ask, brow furrowing in confusion.

"Yes," she says, eyes pleading. "But I didn't do anything to your dad. I wouldn't. I loved him. I found out after that Jasper broke into his house and suffocated him while he was sleeping. He put the pills next to his bed so it looked like he overdosed. I'm so sorry, Bronte. I now have to play along with Jasper because he's still threatening my daughter. I don't know what to do. He thinks I'm allied with him when really I hate him and want him out of my life. I'm in the process of moving Anne to a different college in another state, somewhere he can't find her."

I don't know if I should believe her or not. She could easily be saving her own ass here, and hoping that we only target Jasper now, not her.

I'm not sure what to think. I heard her conversations with Jasper, but if she's playing him, then she would have said whatever she needed to keep him happy.

My dad was suffocated while he slept.

The thought horrifies me.

What a coward of a man Jasper is. I never thought I could hate someone as much as I do him.

"I'm so sorry about your dad, Bronte. He used to talk about you so much, and he cared so much what you thought of him. He wanted to be the best dad in the world, and he wanted to give you everything. It's my fault he's gone. If Jasper didn't see him with me and thought he had an in with me... If he hadn't stolen the key from me, the one your dad gave me for his house…" She starts to cry.

So that's how he got inside the house.

"How do I know all of this is the truth, and it's not just you freaking out and trying to get away with the fact that people who love my dad are now going to want revenge?" I say very plainly.

"I *was* freaking out," she admits. "But mostly because I didn't want you to think that I did this. I loved Freddy. And I might not be the perfect woman, or person, but I'm not capable of killing someone, especially someone I love. I couldn't live with myself if you thought that. I have no criminal record whatsoever—if you look into me the only thing you will find is me being brought in beaten and filing a criminal charge against Jasper."

"What happened to Billie?" I ask.

She looks down, swallowing hard. "Jasper shot her. He thought she was you and took the chance. I wasn't there, but Jasper called me when I was at the studio and told me that maybe I was right, that people are looking into him and know what happened. He's paranoid now, which makes him even more dangerous."

At the studio, so it was a conversation we missed. I don't know whether or not she knows about us bugging her car and home, but she seems oblivious. That, or she's just a really damn good liar, which is a huge possibility.

I try to read her, but she gives nothing away, and I have no idea what to believe.

"I don't know what to say right now," I whisper.

"But I can see why my dad didn't introduce you to me. I would have been able to tell him you weren't worth his time just by meeting you."

Pain flashes in her eyes, and she averts her gaze.

And for a second, I regret my words, but then I remember that without her, I would still have my dad.

She leaves my workplace without a word, and I let her.

But now I'm more confused than ever.

## Chapter Twenty

A few nights later we invite Heidi over to my apartment for dinner. I make a roast chicken, potato salad, garlic bread and a salad with spinach, feta, cucumber and tomato. I might not be a master chef, but I can make do.

Crow tells me how he owns the house Heidi lives in. "So you bought it as an investment house?" I ask, popping a piece of feta in my mouth.

"I bought it for me to have a little privacy if need be, but I never ended up using it because I'm always at the clubhouse. I was going to rent it out, but then Heidi's lease came to an end and she was freaking out, so I told her she could just move into my place," he explains, turning the tap on to wash the sink of dishes that's accumulated.

"You're a good brother," I say.

"What are you going to do with the house?" he asks, lining the plates up neatly.

I shrug. "Rent it out, I guess. I was thinking maybe I could so something nice for someone, like rent it out to a single parent for cheap or something. I don't want to live in it, but I don't want to get rid of it either."

"And the money?"

"I don't know," I admit, biting my bottom lip. "I really don't. I do know I need to give back in some way. I don't want all of that money—it's money off other people's addictions—and I don't think I can ever be okay with that."

I know Dad did it for me, but I can't accept that. It just wouldn't feel right.

Heidi arrives wearing red tartan leggings and a black crop. "Love your place," she says as she steps inside with a bottle of champagne. "These apartments are all so new and modern."

"Thank you," I say, beckoning her inside. She hands me the cold bottle of alcohol, and I thank her again.

She turns to her brother and flashes him a big grin. "So this is where you've been hiding out recently?"

"Something like that," he replies, giving her a hug. "What have you been up to?"

"Nothing much," she admits as we head to the kitchen to pour us all some champagne. "I enrolled into another course for next semester, but until then I'm just going to chill."

"You could get a job," Crow suggests in a dry tone, standing next to me and leaning forward over the counter. "You could even work at Kamikaze."

"I don't have any bar experience," she says, frowning. "I want to be a doula and help people give birth. I don't want to serve drinks to drunk, sleazy men."

I have no idea what a doula is, but I know I'm going to search it online when she leaves. "If you don't work, how do you…live?" I ask, even though I think I already know the answer.

She smiles widely at her brother. "Crow gave me a debit card, so I just use that whenever I need anything."

I slowly bring my eyes to Crow, who avoids my gaze. "Really? So he paid for your vacation and everything?" I'm assuming she lives in his house and he covers all the mortgage and bills.

I realize that Heidi is very spoiled, and that Crow must have paved the way for that. He's obviously a very doting big brother, and she's all he has, as his parents live overseas. It's not really my business how he wants to spend his money and support his sister, but surely this plan isn't sustainable? Maybe it's just like the olden days and she'll rely on him until she gets married, and then her husband can support her.

Hey, who am I to judge? I have drug money coming my way soon.

"Yeah, that was for my birthday present, though," she says, taking the glass I hand to her and lifting it in the air. "To my brother and his beautiful new girlfriend. I never thought the day would come when he'd meet someone he actually enjoyed spending time with for more than just sex. Welcome to the family, Bronte."

I almost choke on my champagne, but manage to cover it up and swallow.

I mean, it was a compliment, right?

"Thanks, Heidi," he groans, and looks to me with apologetic eyes. "I'm sorry."

"Always nice to know I'm not just a walking vagina," I reply, shaking my head at him. Just how much of a playboy was he before me? Maybe he just liked a lot of casual flings.

The past is the past, though, and I'm the one who gains from his vast experience. At least that's what I tell myself.

We all sit down, and Crow helps me set out all the food.

"This looks amazing," Heidi says, checking out all of the options. "I can't remember the last time I had a home-cooked meal."

Of course she eats out every day.

We all dig in and Heidi tells us all about her vacation in Hawaii. "It was amazing. You guys should totally go there on your honeymoon."

She definitely doesn't have a filter, and I find myself laughing at some of her comments.

"Think we're a little way off that," I reply, arching my brow at Crow.

I would love to marry him one day, but we have a few loose ends to tie before we can even think of anything like that.

He just laughs in reply. "Hey, you never know." I do love that he doesn't freak out about it, though.

"Tell me everything about you, Bronte," Heidi says, smiling warmly at me. "I always wanted a sister."

And just like that, I know why Crow gives her everything. She's warm and sweet and makes you feel good about yourself.

Hell, she can take my money, too.

## Chapter Twenty-One

"I didn't know you were so into baking," I say to Nadia, watching her make up batches of brownies, muffins and pizza rolls. "Can you meal prep for me?"

"I've only just gotten into it," she admits, whizzing around my kitchen. "And yes, I'll make all of this for you and you can freeze it, just pull it out when you want them. How good is it?"

"Pretty damn good."

"Where's Crow tonight?" she asks as she makes dough from scratch.

"He's at the clubhouse doing biker stuff. I told him I'm going to have a girls' night, and I'm sure he wants to spend some time with his brothers," I say.

Knock, knock.

"Who's that?" she asks, washing her hands in the sink.

"I have no idea," I reply, picking up my phone and logging into my security app to see who's there. "It's my uncle."

After rushing to the door, I let him in and hug him

as he passes me. "Hey. Is everything okay? You're not usually one to drop in unannounced."

I feel like I have to ask everyone this more than I should. Any time someone comes around now, I automatically assume that something has gone wrong, and with good reason.

"I got your voice mail about Jean dropping into your work and I thought I'd come and talk to you about it," he says, and says hello to Nadia as he spots her.

"I was telling Bronte I think they need to place a security guard in front of there, because I don't like how she just walked in," Nadia says to him, frowning.

"I agree," he replies.

"Yeah, you're right. Crow mentioned the same thing. What do you think about what she had to say?" I ask as we all sit down on my couch. "Do you think she's genuine?"

"I don't know what to do about Jean. I think you should decide, and let me know."

Me?

Shit.

I asked to be involved, and I guess this is him handing me the reins.

"What if what she says is the truth? She's clearly not the best person out there, but I don't know if she deserves to…die."

There, I said it.

These people aren't just going away on fucking vacation, they are being killed in retaliation for what they've done. And there's no point pretending otherwise.

"Did you check up on what she said? We should check the records and see if the domestic abuse is true," I suggest.

"Already did, and it is," Nadia states, shrugging. "And she was married to him, and she does have a college-age daughter named Anne."

"So everything is true, except we just don't know if she's lying about her involvement with Dad's death. Can we find out if she really is moving her daughter to a different college? Maybe Jean will move there with her and we won't have to worry about her anymore," I say, thinking that would be a best-case scenario.

It's clear I'm leaning toward having a little faith and trusting her. If everything else she said was true, there's a chance all of it was. Jasper is a hundred-percent guilty, but with Jean, I don't know if she is, so of course I'm not going to want anything to happen to her.

"So you want us to let her be?" Neville nods, leaning back and studying me. "We can find out about the college thing, if need be. But if that's what you want to do, then okay." He leans forward and kisses my head. "And please go and see your dad's lawyer. He won't stop calling me, trying to get you to go in there."

"I will," I promise.

Eventually.

"I did see him at the station, but I didn't have time to discuss the will with him."

"I better get going, I didn't mean to interrupt your girls' night," he murmurs, standing up and fixing his navy suit. "Let me know if you need anything, or if there's any kind of trouble."

Nadia comes over with a container filled with baked goods. "For you."

"Thank you, Nadia," he replies with a smile, then turns to me. "I don't know what's going to happen next, but we will find out. I'm going after Jasper, so shit will hit the fan really soon. Just stay safe, Bronte."

"I will."

He leaves and I make sure the apartment is all locked up.

"Your life has so much more drama than mine does," Nadia announces, shaking her head and going back into the kitchen. "I don't know how you do it. Here, eat a cookie, you deserve one."

I eat a few cookies, and then I text Crow and tell him my uncle dropped in, and that everything is fine.

At least I hope it is.

Abbie comes to visit at work, answering phones for me in between our chats. "So what else has been going on with you? Dad said he dropped in to see you the other night," she says, tapping a pen on her lips.

"He did. We discussed the current plan." I don't know how much she knows, but I'm assuming whatever the Knights know, they let her in on.

"I heard," she admits, lowering her voice. "Temper is staying on alert."

"I told him to not worry about Jean. I don't think she'll give us any more trouble."

And so far, she hasn't. No one has seen or heard from her, although she must have realized we bugged her car and house, because the bugs were destroyed. So we can no longer listen to her personal conversations.

"I don't know how you all live in a state of permanent stress," I say, resting my forehead against the cold wooden table. "Like, what is going to happen next? Is Jean going to come out of nowhere and prove me wrong? Is Jasper still alive or being held captive and tortured somewhere?"

Cam walks by and I instantly shut up, not wanting her to get involved in all of this. "James is coming now for those parts. Can you send him into the garage to see me when he does?"

"Sure," I reply, smiling. "Anything else?"

"Yeah, you look good in red," she adds, grinning and walking off.

"She's not wrong," Crow says as he approaches. He's wearing another bowling shirt, yellow and blue this time, and it's particularly terrible.

"How many of those shirts do you own?" I ask, wishing the one he's wearing now would die in a fire.

"A lot," he replies, smirking. "Remind me to show you the next time you come to the clubhouse."

"He has a whole wardrobe full of them," Abbie

agrees, eying it in distaste. "I don't know how you get women in them, really."

"Ask Bronte," he says, leaning down and kissing me. "The only woman I want."

I touch his stubbled cheeks with my fingers. "I better be the only woman that you want."

"Get a room, you two," Abbie adds, pulling us back away from each other and inserting herself between us. A few customers walk in and we all go into professional mode.

Crow winks at me as he walks away, and Abbie and I share a look. "You're crazy about him, aren't you?"

Sighing, I reply, "You have no idea. Or I guess you do. I want to be around him all the time, but then I remind myself that I'm an independent woman and I don't need no man."

Abbie starts laughing, her shoulders shaking. "I know exactly what you mean. I don't know what I'd do without Temper—he's everything to me. He's my family, my lover, and I know he will always have my back and be loyal to me. I know that you and Crow haven't been together long, but soon you'll realize you can be both head over heels in love with your man, and still a strong-ass woman."

"You're very wise," I say, watching as Crow speaks to the new customers, making one of the women laugh at something. "And he's too damn charming for his own good."

"He is, isn't he? But he's all yours. Trust me when I say you have nothing to worry about. Besides, I live with him and I'd personally kick his ass if anything shady went on."

We fist bump.

"Speaking of, I'm thinking of having a party at the clubhouse next weekend. It's been a while since everyone has been together, so what do you think? Want to lose your biker party virginity?" she asks, wiggling her eyebrows.

"I'm there," I reply instantly.

Crow leaves work early to head to Kamikaze, and when George, my dad's lawyer, calls me for the millionth time, this time I answer and tell him I will drop by his office after I finish work. When I get there, I can tell he's extremely unhappy with me.

"I've tried to contact you so many times," he says, sitting opposite me, scowling over the desk, tapping the paperwork so it's in line. "Your dad had a very clear will, everything goes to you. His house, his money, his cars, everything. And it's a substantial amount of money."

"How much?" I ask.

He slides me a piece of paper and, eying him, I lift it up and look at the amount.

Holy shit.

Business must have been pretty damn lucrative. My dad never bought anything flashy or designer, or lived out of his means. He was just a normal guy in a normal house with a normal car, or at least that's what I thought.

"Wowzer" is all I can manage to say.

So I'm a millionaire now. Something I never thought in my wildest dreams would ever happen to me. I don't even know what I'm going to do with this money, but it feels like a lot of pressure.

George makes me sign some documents and gives me all the details that I need to know.

"Thank you," I say, standing up and offering him my hand. "And sorry for being such a pain in the ass. Being here just made it all real, you know?"

And I never wanted it to be real.

He nods. "He was a good man."

"I know," I say, offering him a sad smile.

I walked into his office with five hundred dollars in my account and I'm leaving with just over a million to my name. As I step outside, I look up at the sky.

"And I'd give it all away in a second just to have you back for one day, Dad."

## Chapter Twenty-Two

"Hey," Crow says with his phone pressed against his ear. "Okay, just take whatever you need from my card. Stay safe, you hear me? Okay, bye."

I mustn't be able to hide my expression because he tilts his head and asks, "What?"

"Nothing. Just wishing I had a sibling like you who would make my life extremely easy," I say, smirking.

"I know, I've spoiled her," he grumbles, sitting back down next to me on the couch. "But you know our parents aren't here—they are off enjoying their empty nest, living their best lives—so I make sure I'm there for her. I'm in a lucky position where I don't have to worry too much about finances, so of course I want to make sure she's taken care of. Does it annoy you?"

"It's your money," I say, lifting my legs up and laying them over his. "But…"

"I knew there was a but."

I grin. "There's always a but. She's never going to learn to be independent, or hardworking, or any of those things if you just give her everything."

"Yeah, I suppose those are important qualities," he says in a dry tone. "It's just always been this way, and she's used to it. I don't know how she'd do without my money, if I'm being honest."

"You don't have to cut her off. Maybe just make her get a job or something. I don't know, it's up to you, but that's what I'd do," I admit.

We head to work, and I happily sit down at my desk when we get there. "You're lucky I love my job here," I say to Crow.

"Why?"

"Because I can afford not to work now, so if I hated it here, I could quit in some dramatic-ass way. Maybe knock over a motorcycle or something," I joke, closing the desk drawer.

Crow just smirks, crossing his arms over his bright green T-shirt, accentuating his strong biceps. "Well, lucky is the right word then, isn't it? Considering you basically run the place now, and it would probably fall apart without you."

I've really gotten the hang of this whole admin thing, and I love organizing everything for the business. The new staff members, Pia and Alex, have taken over customer service and helping sell the merchandise, and know way more than me about all the bike parts, leaving me to simply do reception, which has been way less stressful. It's also meant that I can properly do all the bookkeeping and accounts and handle the phones.

"I'm glad you are aware of that." With no one else

around, I go to him and steal a sneaky kiss. "The eye candy around here is pretty good, too."

"I was just thinking the same thing," he murmurs, holding on to my neck and bringing me in for another kiss. "But it's also very distracting. I find myself looking over at you constantly, wondering what you're doing."

"I'm usually doing the exact same thing," I laugh. "Sitting at the computer, or I'm on the phone."

"Yeah, and you're looking sexy while doing it," he says as he nuzzles my neck. "And fuck, you smell so good, too. If no one was here right now, I'd lift you up on that desk and—"

"You two just can't help yourselves, can you?" Cam asks, making me jump. She is standing in front of my desk and blowing a big bubble with her gum. "I need you for a moment, Crow. There's a problem with one of the bike parts—I think we've ordered in the wrong part."

"Coming," he replies.

"You might have been if I didn't wander over," she replies in a dry tone, laughing at her own joke.

I spend the next hour on the phone ordering parts for the next few custom motorcycles and organizing the business receipts to send to the accountant.

When it's closing time, I still have a little work to do, so I decide to stay behind and just get everything done. My new reorganization system is almost complete, and I just want to keep going until it's all sorted. An hour later and it is, and I'm about to leave the garage, opening the door, when I see a man right in front of me. He pushes past me through the door, overpowering me as I try to shove him back outside.

I've never seen this man in person, but I know who he is from pictures. Jasper. And I know that right now I'm in deep shit.

What is he doing here? Hasn't he done enough already?

He looks like crap, with bags under his eyes, messy hair and rumpled clothes. He has desperation written all over him, and that makes him more dangerous than ever.

"What the hell are you doing?" I ask, the hair on the back of my neck standing on end.

This can't be good.

I know this isn't going to end well for me.

"Close the door," he demands, beady dark eyes on me as he pulls out a gun out and aims it at me. "Now. And I'm not fucking around. Listen to what I say or you are going to die. Just like your father died."

Shit.

Him mentioning my dad makes my blood turn to ice, and I've never wanted revenge on someone more than I do right now. This man is a complete piece of shit. A coward.

And I'm not going to let him get what he wants right now.

I'm going down fighting.

I close the door and face him, just the two of us, alone in this huge garage. "What do you want, Jasper?"

I try to stay calm. Panicking isn't going to help the situation, and I don't want anything to set him off.

He tilts his head to the side and laughs. "So you know who I am? Well, let me see, Bronte. What do I want?"

He's clearly insane. There's a look in his eyes that says that something has pushed him over the edge.

"I want you dead," he says, finger on the trigger. "I thought I had accomplished that, but instead I killed your little friend. Has anyone ever told you both that you kind of look alike? Unfortunately for her."

I freeze. I knew he did it, but to hear it coming from his mouth so nonchalantly is a whole different story. So he thought Billie was me. She really did die because of me.

I hold my hands up. "You don't need to do this, Jasper. Do you really want more enemies by killing me?"

"I do," he says, sighing. "You've been standing in my way of getting what I want for too long now. And after Jean spoke to you, both her and Anne went missing. What did you say?"

"Nothing," I say, wondering how the hell I'm going to get out of this. "She came to tell me that she didn't kill my dad, that it was all you."

He laughs without humor. "Of course she did. After I kill you, I'm going to get your uncle and then I'll be right where I deserve to be, sitting on top of a drug empire. One by one my enemies will die. No hard feelings, right?"

His finger moves on the trigger, and I'm not going

to stand here and wait to be shot, so I do the only thing I can right now: I run.

I run through the garage, and he shoots two bullets at me, but lucky for me, he misses. He doesn't know this warehouse like I do, and that's the only thing I have going for me right now. I hide in the garage behind a car Crow is working on for fun, and try to control my breathing. I've never been one for guns or weapons, but right now I'm wishing I were a little better equipped to handle a situation like this.

I didn't prepare myself, and now I'm going to die.

I find a tool set and pull out a big wrench. Now if only I can dodge the bullets, maybe I can hit him with this and then run away.

A big bang has me lifting my head, and then I hear Crow's voice yelling my name. "Bronte? Where are you?"

I stand up and slowly walk out, wrench still in hand, body on alert. "I'm here."

"Oh thank God," he says, running to me and pulling me into his arms. "Can you feel my heart? Fuck, I don't think I've ever been so scared in my life."

I look over to see Temper standing there with Jasper lying on the floor, his foot on his back, Jasper's gun in his hand.

"What do you want to do?" Temper asks me, eyes on Jasper.

"What do you mean?" I reply, frowning. "Call the cops."

"You sure you don't want to handle this ourselves?" he asks, lifting his head.

I look to Crow, my mind working. I know they are against this, but I think right now this is the best option for us all. "Call the cops."

He nods, and pulls out his phone.

I don't want them to get into any trouble because of me. My revenge can be him behind bars.

"The cops are on the way, everything will be fine," Crow says, wrapping his arms around me.

"How did you know?" I ask, brow furrowing.

"We have a live camera feed," Crow says, taking the wrench from my hand. "We have a control room and someone always checks to make sure everything is running smoothly. One of the new prospects was on duty, saw you and called me right away. Temper and I were on our way somewhere else and got here as soon as we could."

"He was going to kill me," I say, my body starting to shake. "Just look me in the eye and kill me."

"I know," he replies, jaw tight. "But you're safe, all right? And he's going to be arrested."

Crow needed to save me again. Next time something happens, I want to save my damn self.

The police come and take Jasper away. Temper hands over the security footage of the night, and that's all the proof they will need to lock him away.

"He admitted to killing Billie because he thought she was me," I say to Crow, tears pooling in my eyes. "It really was my fault."

And I don't know how I'm going to live with that.

"Did you get shot?" Crow suddenly asks, touching my skirt.

"No, why?" I ask, frowning. I glance down and see blood.

And then everything goes black.

I wake up in the hospital, Crow sitting on a chair next to my bed, him holding my hand. My mind is fuzzy for a little while, and then everything that happened comes back to me.

Jasper.

Billie.

Crow coming to save me from being next on Jasper's list.

What I don't remember, though, is how I got here, or why I'm even here.

"What happened to me?" I ask Crow, my voice groggy.

I try to sit up, but Crow stands and gestures for me to rest again. "You fainted," he replies, his voice raspy. He avoids my gaze, and by that action I know something is wrong.

"Why won't you look at me?" I ask, squeezing his hand. "Crow, it's me. Whatever it is, just tell me. Did Jasper get away?"

He shakes his head. "No, babe, this has nothing to do with Jasper."

"Then what?" I press.

"You had a miscarriage," he says, voice hitching. He sits back down and finally looks me in the eyes, and I can see how red they are.

He's been crying.

I've never seen Crow cry before.

It takes me a few seconds to process what he just said. A miscarriage? "I was pregnant?" I ask, blinking slowly.

He nods, his Adam's apple bobbing as he swallows. "The stress of what happened with Jasper..."

I was pregnant, and I had a miscarriage. And I didn't even know that I was, so I couldn't even enjoy the moment, or the surprise.

When will Jasper stop taking from me?

Covering my face with my hands, I take a few deep breaths.

How cruel this world can be. All I've ever wanted is to be a mother, and just as I had given up on that idea, I was given what I'd always wanted and also had it taken away on the same day. I didn't even know if I could ever get pregnant, especially while on the pill, and now I've landed myself in this mess.

I don't even know what to say right now. I'm speechless.

How much can one person take?

I didn't even know I was pregnant, and now my obsession with finding Dad's killer has made me lose the one thing that might have made me feel whole again.

When I cry, Crow cries with me.

Nothing else could have kicked me more while I was already down.

## Chapter Twenty-Three

Later that week, I sit on the floor in the shower, just replaying that night in my head. What could I have done differently? What would have happened if Crow and Temper hadn't shown up? What if I didn't stay late at work? Would I still have lost my baby?

The guilt and regret and the what-ifs are just eating me inside.

Crow comes in with a glass of red wine and I turn off the shower, hop out and drink it greedily. "Thank you."

"You're welcome. Anything else I can get you?" he asks, pushing my hair back off my face and staring down at me. "How are you? Don't shut me out—I need you to talk to me and let us get through this together."

It was his baby, too, and I know he's just as sad as I am. Maybe because he knew how much I wanted it, and how much shit life has shoveled at me this month alone.

Maybe because he wanted it, too.

I nod. "I will be. I just can't stop thinking about it and wishing I never stayed late."

"I know," he whispers. "But we don't know what could have happened. He might have followed you, and we might have even lost you. We just can't think like that, okay? You're fine, and that's all that matters to me. I don't know what would have happened if I lost you, Bronte. I *can't* lose you."

I know exactly how he feels, because without him, I would be incomplete.

"It just hurts, so badly," I whisper.

"I know," he replies, kissing my temple. "I know. I wish I could take the pain away from you. I'd do that in a heartbeat. I'd carry all the pain for the both of us."

I believe him.

"I don't even know how I got pregnant," I say. "I'm sorry, Crow. I told you I couldn't and then this happened...and—"

"You have nothing to be sorry about," he says to me.

"The doctor said there was a low chance that I'd get pregnant because of everything going on, with my problems with ovulation and being on the pill. It was such a small probability he didn't even think it'd happen. He also said..."

"What?" he asks, squeezing my hand.

"He says the abnormal cells have returned even though I only had the surgery months ago," I say, swallowing hard as I try not to get emotional about it.

"Bronte—"

"I've accepted that was a possibility. The abnormal

cells just keep returning, and there's only so many times they will remove them before wanting to take the next step. But now, after knowing I can get pregnant... Maybe I could put it off. I don't know. Maybe there's a little hope for me?"

"Babe, you need to tell the doctor to do what they need to do to keep you safe," he says, scanning my eyes. "They know best. We can worry about everything else later. Right now, I just need *you* safe. Do you understand me?"

"I do."

And he's right, there's no point putting all of this off.

But it *hurts*.

I was so close to getting what I've always wanted, and with a man I love more than anything.

I know it's not just me in this relationship, though.

"Would you want a baby with me?" I blurt out, realizing I've never even asked him how he's feeling right now.

"Of course I would," he replies, brow furrowing. "There's no one I'd rather have as the mother of my child, and I know that's what you've always wanted. But my number one priority is you, Bronte. Without you, my whole world is gone. Later, we can worry about babies. We have a lot of time to figure out what is right for us. What's meant to be will be. Right now, though, I just need my woman safe."

I wrap my arms around him and cry into his neck. I know his words make perfect sense, but they don't make it hurt any less. I'm giving up something important to me.

But he's right, I need to be here, and I need to follow the medical advice given to me.

"I'll speak to the doctor," I say after I've stopped crying.

"Good," he whispers, sounding relieved.

"And Crow, thank you for always having my back," I say. "I never understood the term ride or die until right now. And I never knew that anyone other than my family, people who are blood related to me, would ever be there for me on this level, and that I could trust someone entirely like I trust you."

His eyes fill with love. "I'm crazy about you. Of course I'm going to do anything to look after you and make sure you're going to be here, right by my side."

I drink half the glass of wine. "I have to admit, I didn't see this one coming. It's hard to mourn something that was such a surprise, but here I am."

And it hurts so damn much, I don't even know how I'm functioning right now.

"It would have been the best surprise, but it wasn't meant to be. That doesn't mean we won't get our time, our happily ever after with a family," he says, kissing me and then leaving me to get dressed. My life has never had so much going on in it before, not even when I was Nadia's assistant, and I don't know how I keep getting myself into trouble.

It's like just when you think something is over, something else pops up. My dad would have said that anything that happens, anything that scares you, is character building.

The problem is, I don't know who I'm going to turn into if my life keeps going like this. I don't want to lose who I am, but I'm going to need to adapt, become harder and stronger.

Crow is like a superhero, and I'm not even at side-kick level yet.

"Crow!" I call out.

"Yeah?" he replies, sticking his head into my bedroom. "More wine?"

I smile. "I'd love some more wine, but that's not why I called you. I was wondering, could you teach me how to shoot a gun?"

He studies me for a few seconds, mind working, before he replies, "Yeah, I can teach you how to shoot a gun."

"And some self-defense?" I press.

He nods. "Of course. Anything else?"

"Yeah," I reply. "Can you come and keep me warm?"

He smiles and steps into the room fully, pulling off his T-shirt and showing off that beautiful body of his. I watch as he slinks around the room, removing his shoes and putting them in the corner with his clothes, until he's naked and slides into the bed next to me, kissing my cheek.

He just holds me all night, and it's just what I need.

"I'm so sorry he got to you before we got to him," Neville says, reaching over and touching my arm. I didn't tell him about the miscarriage, because he feels guilty enough, and I know how that feels.

I wouldn't wish it on anyone.

Apparently Uncle Neville had planned on storming into Jasper's house the next morning and taking him down.

The next morning.

That's how unlucky I am.

There was a holdup because Jasper had left town and no one could locate him for a few days there. He had only returned the same day he came after me at the garage.

I think we underestimated him.

"It's not your fault," I say. "And he's behind bars now, so that's something. I hope he gets put away for a very long time."

"He will be. And when he gets out…let's just say I'm someone who likes to hold a grudge," he replies in a dry tone.

"What's happening with your…business?"

He hesitates before answering. "After recent events, I can't trust that my family will be left unharmed if I walk away. I don't think there is any walking away in this…line of work. On the top is the only place that's safe for me. I don't know what I'm going to do yet, but trying to retire made me lose my only sibling, and I don't want to lose anything or anyone else. Right now I have power. The power to protect Abbie, and you, and anyone else I love. If I let go of that, I don't know what will happen. I'm trapped."

I can see it from his point of view. I guess it would

be hard to walk away. He'd probably have to leave the city and move somewhere else, somewhere where no one would know him. "You do whatever you need to do. But I'm always here if you need something."

He smiles at me like I'm being cute, but I do mean it. "I appreciate that, Bronte."

"Your daughter is dropping in for lunch tomorrow if you want to come and eat with us," I say. "We've all never caught up properly before. I think we need to start doing that."

"I agree," he says. "I'd love to have lunch with you both."

He leaves, promising to return tomorrow, and as I continue working on my computer, one thought crosses my mind.

Is life going to be normal now?

Crow walks in, another bright printed shirt spread across his large, muscular body. "Babe, you want to go for a quick ride? Prez wants me to go and pick up something, and I thought we could go to the range and have a shoot. You wanted to learn, and I'm going to teach you."

I grin.

I don't think my life with a Knight is ever going to be normal, and I love that.

I love him.

The next few months just whizz by. I get the payout from my dad's will, I rent out his house, and I make a huge donation in his name to the children's hospital. I give a chuck of money to Nadia, so she doesn't have to stress over money anymore and can keep her business going. She initially refused, but then only agreed when I became a silent partner. So now I partially own the business that I was laid off from. Crazy how life works, right?

I try to give some to Abbie, but she declines, telling me she has enough money. Jasper ended up in prison, serving a long sentence for murder, and Jean is safely out of town with her daughter.

"Do you feel safer now?" Nadia asks me, sitting at my work desk at Fast & Fury and eating carrot sticks and hummus.

"I do," I admit to her. "But I also feel even safer knowing I can now operate a firearm and do basic self-defense. If something happens, I can try to fight back, not just have to run away like last time and hope for the best."

I'll never allow myself to be that weak and vulnerable again. I learned that the women at the MC all know basic fighting skills, and they all know how to shoot a gun. I think it's left me feeling a little more confident now, and I will continue to take classes to keep getting better and toning up my new skills.

Crow comes up behind me and places his hands on my shoulders, massaging the knots there.

He's been my saving grace through this whole thing. He has pulled me through the depression after losing the baby, something I still struggle with every day, but I'm still able to smile, to go to work, and to enjoy my life.

And I owe that all to him, and my own strength.

# Chapter Twenty-Four

*Three Years Later*

"Quinn Frieda Billie Crow," I say out loud, looking at the little bundle in my arms. She might not be of our blood, but I love her just like I would my own, and have since the moment I found out we were going to be adopting her. "She's so cute, Crow. I can't even deal right now."

"I know," Crow agrees, kissing the bottom of her little foot. "She's perfect."

I did end up having to have a hysterectomy about eighteen months ago. I wasn't ready to give up my dream of being a mother, especially when Crow and I got married soon after Jasper was sentenced. It was my dream outdoor wedding, to my dream man, and I always knew that we would expand our little family somehow. Adoption ended up being the option we went with. We applied as soon as I had my surgery, knowing it could take some time. Crow was on board from the beginning, and he has never held it against me for me being unable to give him a biological child, or ever made me feel any less of a woman.

I love him for that. He has been so amazing through the whole thing, so patient and open to all options and avenues.

When we contacted an adoption agency, we were told it would be a long process. We were lucky enough that a young mother chose us to be the parents of her beautiful little girl. We saw Quinn's birth, something I will never forget, and now we get to take her home. Molly, Quinn's biological mother, wanted a closed adoption, and we've given her that. I know the time will come when Quinn will get older and want answers, and I need to prepare myself for that, but for right now, we get to raise this beautiful little girl as our own. I've never loved anyone more.

It's crazy how life can change. I couldn't be happier right now, with my dream man and a beautiful daughter of my own.

Crow kisses me and then opens his arms. "Are you going to share her?"

"I guess," I grumble, handing her over to him. "I'm just so in love with her, it's hard to even let her out of my arms."

"I know exactly what you mean," he says to her in a baby voice. "You are going to be so loved, little Quinn."

Abbie and Temper drop in that evening, and Temper gives me a stack of money as a baby present. "You don't have to give me money, Temper," I say, looking to Crow. "That's a lot of money. You know a card or something would have been fine."

He waves his arm. "This is a Knight baby, and we're all going to make a big deal. Use the money for whatever you want. Start a bank account for her. Take her to Disneyland. Whatever."

"Disneyland?" I repeat, laughing. "I'd love to take her to Disneyland Paris one day. This would cover the trip."

"There you go. Perfect," he replies, grinning.

"You know Abbie already bought us a lot of stuff and wouldn't take the money for it."

"There will be plenty more coming," Abbie adds, slowly rocking Quinn.

"She looks good with a baby," I say to Temper, arching my brow. "A little too good."

"I was thinking the same thing," Temper replies, rubbing the back of his neck.

Abbie's cheeks start to redden. "Calm down there, let's not get ahead of ourselves."

Temper holds Quinn next, and he looks so awkward I can't help but laugh. However, the big, burly man is so gentle with her. It's adorable to watch.

After Abbie and Temper leave, Nadia and Cam drop in, and then my uncle. Once they're all gone we order in some food and brace ourselves for Night Two with a newborn. When Crow suggests I have a little me time, I take a long, relaxing bath, using my new Baby Yoda bath bomb, closing my eyes and thinking about how goddamn wonderful my life is right now.

When the water turns cold I get out of the bath,

dress in some pajamas and find Crow and Quinn in the living room. She's asleep on his chest and he's watching reruns of *Supernanny* on TV.

"Taking notes?" I ask, smirking.

"Actually, I am. Our daughter is going to be nothing like these little kids," he proclaims, wincing as a little girl hits her mom. "Yeah, there'll be none of that. She's going to show respect and not be a little brat."

I sit down next to him. "You know all toddlers are naughty, though, right?"

"Yeah, but there's naughty and then there's that," he says, pointing at the screen with the remote. "Does this time-out thing really work?"

Feeling amused, I watch him freak out a little at all things parenting. "We'll be fine, Crow. And so will she."

"With you as her mother, I have no doubt," he says, turning his head to look at me. "And with her beauty, I'm also probably going to end up in prison at some point, but you know what? I was probably headed there anyway."

Shaking my head at him, I can't help but laugh at that. "No one is going to prison. We need you here."

Quinn starts to fuss, so I take her to change and feed her, letting Crow have a little time to himself. Is this what parenting is? Tag teaming so much you barely see each other or get to spend any time together or do anything as a couple?

No wonder only the strong survive.

"But you, miss, are an angel sent from heaven," I say, smelling her. "And you smell so good."

She holds on to my thumb with her little fingers.

I don't care if she keeps me up all night for the rest of my life.

She is so worth it.

"Crow, can you take your daughter, please? She pooped again," I grumble, my voice thick with sleep.

"So now she's my daughter?" he asks, laughing to himself. "Come here, Quinn, let me change you."

"I never realized how much I was taking sleep for granted before this," I say with my eyes closed. It's been a week since I had a good night of it. "Broken sleep should be considered a reason to not have to go into work. It feels like shit."

"Go back to sleep, Bronte, I have her," he says, and I don't need to be told twice. I fall asleep instantly, and when I wake up again the sun is shining.

Forcing myself out of bed, I head to the nursery where Quinn is fast asleep in her crib, while Crow is out in the living room.

Doing push-ups.

Shirtless.

He has a sheen of sweat covering his body, and I find my lips suddenly feeling a little dry. Here I am, looking like crap, and he's still looking like a Greek god first thing in the morning.

"Good morning," I say, enjoying the view. "Are you doing this on purpose? Because you're not really playing fair right now."

He laughs and continues with his workout. "Just

getting some exercise in. Just because I'm a dad now doesn't mean I need to have a dad bod."

I get myself some coffee, and sit down on the couch, pretending to be watching the news, but I'm watching him instead.

He says something, but I miss it because I'm too busy perving to listen. "What?"

"I'm going to go for a quick jog around the block," he repeats.

"Like that? With no shirt on?" I ask, eyes narrowing.

So my whole neighborhood gets to see him like that? Even that woman across the road who likes to check out all the younger guys?

"Yeah, why?" he asks, frowning. "It's warm out. I'll be back in ten minutes."

"Okay," I reply, gritting my teeth.

Well, here's an emotion I haven't felt in a while: jealousy.

"Have fun, you big show-off," I mutter to myself as he leaves. "I could go outside and be all sexy too."

Maybe in a few weeks, when I'm not so exhausted. I don't know how he has the energy for it.

Quinn wakes up and starts screaming blue murder, so I get a bottle ready and give her what she wants. "Good morning to the most special girl in the world. Where's your daddy, you wonder? Well, he's out showing off his ripped body to all the women in the neighborhood."

Quinn opens her eyes wider.

"That was my reaction too, my girl."

\* \* \*

Heidi comes over to spend time with her niece. "She is one beautiful kid," she says, rocking Quinn gently. "And you get to keep your sexy figure. It's a win-win, Bronte."

I laugh at that. "Only you would even think of that, Heidi."

She grins and lifts her head up, looking at me. "So I got a job at Kamikaze. I know I just finished my associate degree, but I also know Crow wants me to get a job. I appreciate you and him letting me take time to go to school. I'm working a few days a week now as a bookkeeper."

"That's awesome news," I say, smiling. Crow had a serious discussion with her and she reacted better than I thought she would, which means I didn't give her enough credit. She asked if she could go to school to figure out what she is good at and Crow was thrilled. "How do you feel about working like the rest of us?"

"It sucks," she admits, pursing her lips. "But the people there are really cool, and I can't just live off Crow forever. He has his own family now, and I need to be a little more independent." She pauses and adds, "Just a little, not completely."

I laugh again. "Well, little steps, so, well done. You should be proud."

"I am." She beams. "And while I do work in the back, being in the club environment is fun. The bartenders even let me play around behind the bar before we open, and I even made up my own cocktail.

Now they're going to sell it at the bar, which is pretty sweet."

"That *is* impressive," I say. "I'll have to try it next time I go there."

"You should. I called it Too Pretty to Work But Still Here Anyway."

My jaw drops. "You didn't?"

She nods.

This time I can't stop laughing. Heidi is a riot. She's spoiled, sure, but she's sweet, and now that I have my own daughter, I know exactly where Crow was coming from. Because I just want to give Quinn everything and never see her struggle a day in her life.

"You're hilarious. Maybe that's your calling. Creating new cocktails with names that make people laugh when they order them."

"A girl can dream."

"Do you want to have kids?" I ask, watching her with Quinn.

"One day, sure," she replies, smiling widely. "But I think I have a long way to go before I can be responsible to care for a baby. I can barely look after myself right now."

"I'm sure with babysitting Quinn, you'll be a pro in no time," I tease.

Crow walks in and stops when he sees us all. "My three favorite girls all in one room. How did I get so lucky?"

Damn, the man is charming.

He comes and sits down, stealing Quinn from his sister. "I heard you had your first day at Kamikaze."

"Yep." Heidi beams.

"And she already created her own drink for the menu," I add, pride in my tone.

Crow looks impressed. "Good on you, Heidi."

"Wait, let her tell you what it's called."

She tells him, and then it's his turn to lose it laughing.

## Chapter Twenty-Five

"What a beautiful baby you have," a girl at the grocery store says to me. She must be in her early twenties, and has beautiful long blond hair. "She is so cute."

"Thank you," I say, smiling. "She's a week old today."

"What's her name?" she asks, unable to take her eyes away.

"Quinn."

"Love that name." She beams. "Well, you both have a good day."

"You too," I reply, waving.

I carry on with my shopping, when Crow calls. "Hey."

"Hey, babe. Where are you?" he asks.

"At the store," I reply. "Why?"

"I'm leaving the clubhouse now and was going to ask if you want anything."

"I'm good. I'll meet you home in twenty."

"Okay," he replies, and we both hang up.

Today is the first day he left our apartment to go

back to the clubhouse, aside from dropping in to get his clothes, and it feels so weird being out and about without him, just with Quinn. I get the last few things I need, check out and head back home.

Quinn starts crying in the back and I feel helpless, knowing I can't even comfort her or feed her while I'm driving, so I pull over into a fast food parking lot. Feeling overwhelmed, I take a breath, feed her and then put her back in her car seat and drive home.

I don't know how single mothers do it, because this whole parenting gig isn't easy.

Crow is already there when I get there, and he comes out and carries the groceries in. I'm glad that he's back, I'm not going to lie. It's so much easier having that extra helping hand and someone you can rely on. It can be stressful knowing that all the responsibility is on you and only you. I much prefer it when he's here with me.

He's on my team, and it's so vital to me right now.

"I had to stop and feed her on the drive home," I say, sitting down on the couch and lifting my feet up. "She was screaming."

"Did you give your mom a hard time?" he says to Quinn as he rocks her. "You should leave her with me and go to the store next time. That will be less stressful for you. Or send me a list, and I'll go."

"I love you," I say, sighing. "Thank you for being here and helping with everything."

He stops in his tracks and turns to me. "I love you, too. And you don't need to thank me, I'm her dad.

This is literally my job to be doing all of this stuff for her, and to support you."

"I really do love you," I say again.

He is such a wonderful father, and it's the biggest turn-on ever.

He bends down and kisses my forehead.

And I close my eyes and enjoy it.


"So guess who contacted me today?" Nadia asks, sitting down on my couch. She came to spend some time with me and Quinn, and I'm happy to have her here.

"Who?" I ask.

"Anne, Jean's daughter. She wants me to help her find her. Apparently she's gone missing or something."

I sit up straighter. "Jean's gone missing?"

In the end Jean was telling the truth about Jasper and her daughter, and she has left us alone since then. I wonder where she is—her poor daughter must be so worried. Her disappearance can't have anything to do with Jasper, who is behind bars, so I have no idea what could have happened to her. Although he might still have people who work for him, so maybe he's calling the shots from prison?

"What are you going to do?" I ask Nadia. "Do you think you can locate her?"

It's so weird to think that if my dad were alive, this news would potentially upset him. It makes me want to help find her, even though he's not even here.

It doesn't really make any sense.

"I could try. What do you think? I don't want to

upset you, so if you don't want me to take this case, I won't."

"If you want to, then go for it," I say. "I don't think Jean is a threat at all, and to be honest, I kind of want to make sure that she's okay."

"I don't either," she agrees. "This whole time we all just assumed they stayed together, but apparently Jean sent Anne off to her new college, set her up, stayed for a while but eventually ended up leaving. She hasn't seen or heard from her since, and Anne is very worried."

"Weird," I mutter. The whole thing makes no sense. I hope she didn't have an accident or something. Or maybe she has a reason she needs to hide out right now. "Where are you going to start with this one?"

Quinn starts fussing in my arms, so I grab her bottle from the coffee table and see if she wants to drink. She does, latching on. "Hungry little girl."

"I'll do an online search and see what I can find, and then go from there. Social media might give me a few clues," Nadia says, shrugging and watching Quinn. "She is so beautiful, Bronte."

"I know." I beam, sighing in contentment. "She is everything I've ever wanted. I'm so lucky Molly picked me to be her mom."

"I think Quinn is the lucky one," Nadia adds, making me smile.

"Do you want some help with this case?" I ask. I'd be lying if I said I didn't miss the private investigator work, and although I love being a mother more than anything, it might be nice to get out of the house and do something else every once in a while. Plus, this case is a little personal, and I wouldn't mind seeing it through.

"Sure. I'll dive in and let you know what I find and we can go from there," she says, holding her arms out as Quinn stops drinking. "Now let me have one more cuddle before I have to go back to work."

Nadia leaves, and I sit down with Quinn, whose blue eyes are looking right at me. "Your granddad would have loved you so much, you know that? His name was Freddy, and he would have spoiled you. He was a good person and a wonderful parent, and hopefully one day you will say the same about me. And your aunt Billie, well, she would have adored you so much, too. And she would have been the one bailing you out of any trouble you got into, and probably not telling me about it. But you know what? They are both looking over us, and they're here with us still. I can feel them."

Quinn farts.

Lovely.

If they are watching over us right now, I'm sure they are both laughing.

## Chapter Twenty-Six

Crow and I decide to have a much-needed day date. With Quinn consuming our lives for the last three months, we've had little to no alone time, and we both want to make sure we make time for ourselves. It's hard leaving a newborn baby, though, and I'm trying not to let my anxiety kick in.

We sit side by side, his arm around me as we wait for our food to arrive. "I still don't know if I made the best choice," I admit, checking the menu. "I went with the prawns but the chicken also looks good."

"If you like mine better, we can swap," he says, kissing my temple.

If that isn't true love, I don't know what is.

"What do you think Quinn is doing?" he asks, picking up his glass of soda and taking a sip. "I hope she's okay."

"I hope Temper and Abbie are okay," I reply in a dry tone, making him laugh. Quinn can be fussy at times, and hard to settle, so I hope she's not putting them off having babies. "She's probably asleep. Do you think you're going to start a trend and all the Knights are going to start having kids now?"

"Maybe—they're all crazy about Quinn. Imagine when she grows up and she has all these scary-ass, tatted biker uncles. No one is ever going to ask her out." He grins, looking extremely happy about it.

"You don't need to look so thrilled," I reply, shaking my head. "If a boy likes her enough, he will still ask her out, so that can be his test."

"What? If he doesn't mind potentially getting killed for her?"

I roll my eyes. "I'm glad we have at least sixteen years until we have to worry about this."

"Eighteen," he replies. "She's not dating until she's eighteen."

"And how old were you?" I ask, raising my brows.

"That's not the point," he fires back, frowning. "She's a girl. And I don't want her to be how I was. She's going to have a better role model in you."

"I started dating when I was like fifteen," I point out to him. "Not that my dad knew—it was all done sneakily. Which is what she will probably do if you don't let her do anything fun."

"She can have fun. Just more like 'board games at home' fun, not 'out drinking with boys' fun," he replies, flashing me his teeth in a grin.

Laughing, I cup his face and look into his eyes. "We'll see how that goes for you, but we have plenty of other stages to get through with her first."

"Luckily." He kisses my lips and then my nose. "I'm so happy right now."

The food arrives and the prawns are placed in front of me. "Me too."

"Because we're on our first date in what feels like forever, or the food?" he asks, and thanks the waitress.

"Both," I reply, grinning.

"Did you get an update from Nadia on Jean?"

"Yeah, no one has heard from her since. She hasn't updated her social media or anything," I say, frowning. "But she's old, so maybe that's why."

Crow smirks. "Maybe she just doesn't use social media. Or maybe she's hiding from someone and doesn't want to be found."

"Who?"

"I don't know, some of Jasper's friends or something. Who knows?" he replies, wrapping his arm around me. "These drug lords have a line of people under them just waiting to do some dirty work."

"If that were true, why would she come back here to the city?" I ask, frowning. "Wouldn't she go as far away from this place as she could instead of running back to it?"

"Yeah, I guess so. There's probably more to the story."

"There always is." I sigh, turning my face to him. "I have kind of missed working for Nadia, though, so it's nice to brainstorm a case with her again."

"Your eyes lit up when you told me about it," he agrees, lip twitching. "Missing the adventure, are you?"

"I love my life and I'm so grateful and blessed to

have both you and Quinn, but yeah, I guess I wouldn't mind a dash of adventure." I pause, and then add, "Just a dash, and someone else's drama, not my own."

He laughs. "That seems fair."

I reach my foot out so it touches his. It's really nice just being here with him, just enjoying each other's company with no other distractions, but at the same time, I really miss my daughter.

Being a parent is weird.

"You playing footsies with me, babe?" he asks, smirking.

"And what if I am?" I ask, arching a brow. "What are you going to do about it?"

"Nothing right now, because that would be frowned upon," he replies, blue eyes filled with amusement. He leans over to whisper in my ear, "But later…"

I clear my throat. "Well, I guess we will see then."

And I can't fucking wait.

We finish up our peaceful, quiet meal, just chatting about everything and anything. It feels nice to have this little break, and to put some extra time into us. We are a happy married couple, but when you bring a child into the world, they become the main focus. It's so easy to forget to look after your partner, and I want to make sure I never do that with Crow. I want him to always feel well loved.

When we head back to the clubhouse, Quinn is fast asleep, so we hang out there for a while, chilling with Temper, Abbie, Renny and Izzy. It's nice to just hang out with them—it feels like so long since we've just sat around and had a drink.

When Quinn wakes up crying, though, I'm happy to hold her, and be with her again, too.

That's what life is about, right? Balance.

My goal is to try to have some of that.

And later that night, after Quinn is fast asleep in her crib, I put in a little effort, dressing in a sexy lace nightie, and sit on the bed, waiting for Crow.

When he steps into the room and sees me, his eyes turn dark with want, and he quickly closes the door behind him.

I can see the outline of his cock through his gray sweatpants, and tell how much he wants me. It's an empowering feeling, knowing that the attraction between us is so strong, and not just physical. It's mental and emotional, too.

"I'm not going to last long with you looking like that," he teases as he pulls off his shirt and throws it on the ground. Everything else follows until he's standing naked in front of me.

"I don't even care," I reply as he comes to the bed, reaching out to touch his cock, stroking it with my hands. I move to the edge of the bed, wanting to drive him crazy, and put my mouth on him. I suck on the head and tease him for a little while, and then I go deeper, taking as much of him as I can into my mouth. I love taking my time with him, and I truly enjoy pleasuring this man. His fingers get lost in my hair, his head leaning back as his mouth drops open in pleasure. I love the growling sounds he makes; they turn me on even more.

"Fuck, Bronte," he breathes, his husky tone making me moan a little around his length. He tries to step back but I hold on to his thighs, pulling him into me. I know he doesn't want this to be over yet, but I want him to come in my mouth, and then we can continue and start again. It's not like he needs much recovery time.

He moans loudly as he comes, and I swallow every drop, and continue to gently suck even when it's over, making his thighs tremble at the sensitivity.

I wipe my mouth and bring my eyes to his.

"That was…fuck" is all he can seem to say with a satisfied smile, followed by, "Your turn."

He pushes me back and lifts up my nightie. Seeing that I'm wearing nothing underneath, he spreads my thighs and slowly starts to feast, returning the favor, teasing me and dragging it out until I'm ready to explode. My back arches as I can feel myself on the verge of coming, and my eyes close of their own accord, lost in the moment and the pleasure.

"Fucking hell, Crow," I moan, spreading my thighs farther apart and lifting my hips. His tongue dashes on my clit at the same time he slides a finger inside of me, and then it's all over for me.

After I've come, we slowly make love with him on top, and then behind me, and then me on top, taking our time and just enjoying being with each other.

Aaaannnd I'm back.


I take Quinn to Dad's headstone. We place flowers down, sit in front of it and just talk to him. I came here today for a reason, and it was to tell him what Nadia and I found out about Jean.

"Jean committed suicide, Dad," I say, sighing. "I don't know how much you cared about her or if you loved her, but I thought you should hear it from me. Her daughter asked Nadia to look for her, and we found her when we were reviewing records of un-identified decedents. Maybe she's sitting with you right now. I don't really know."

I don't know how to feel about the whole thing. I never thought this would be the outcome when we took on this case, and now that we've gotten to the bottom of it, I just feel sad about how it all turned out.

"This is the first time I'm bringing Quinn to your headstone, but I'm going to make sure we come every week at least. I wish you could have held her. She'd have you wrapped around her little finger," I say, smiling sadly. I take a deep breath. "I miss you, Dad, so much. But I know that you are watching over us."

Not too closely, because Crow and I have been all over each other every single night as of recent, and I hope he can't see that.

"And just know that you are so loved, and that you're the best dad I could have ever asked for. I love you. We love you."

We sit there for a while longer, and then move to Billie's headstone. I place her flowers down and talk to her until Quinn gets a little fussy, so we head home. I'm putting her in her car seat when, in a flash, I'm pushed into the back seat, and the door is slammed behind me.

Two people get in the front: a blond woman and a dark-haired man.

"What are you doing? Let us out, please, you can take the car and anything else in it," I beg them, looking at Quinn safely strapped in her car seat. Fear fills me, and I don't know what to do.

They start to drive off, and I could easily jump out, but not with Quinn.

"Help!" I yell, trying to get someone's attention. There is no one close by, and the ones on the other side of the cemetery can't hear me.

"Stay quiet, shut up!" the woman yells. "Or your daughter won't make it."

Pure panic takes over me, and I start to freak out. I figure if they kick me out, maybe it's better to have my daughter in my arms? Letting them drive off with her isn't an option—there's no saying what they would do to her. I unbuckle Quinn's belt but then reconsider. What if they crash the car? I don't know what to do. Which is going to be the safest option for us?

"Please don't hurt her," I say, glancing between them as they speed off. I realize that I recognize the woman—she's the one who came up to us in the grocery store to tell me how cute Quinn was. Has she been following me that entire time? That was months ago.

I pull out my phone and send Crow a quick message. I know that he can track me from my phone. Just in case he doesn't check his, I send the same message on the group chat with all the Knights in there.

Someone will come for me, I know that, but is it going to be in time?

The two of them obviously aren't professional criminals—they didn't take my phone away from me—so I have no idea what they want. They haven't stolen anything. What is their motive?

"Just stay quiet," the woman says. "You'll get what you deserve."

What I deserve?

What have I done to any of them?

I'm missing something, and I need to figure out what it is before it's too late.

What is the connection here?

This has to be one of the boldest kidnappings in broad daylight, but because of Quinn there's not much I can do. I can't fight both of them off, I can't take her and jump, and I can't kick and scream and attack them in case they crash the car and hurt my baby. I'm vulnerable, and they know it.

"I don't even know who you are, but whatever you want, please. I will give it to you, just do not hurt my daughter," I continue, hoping they can get it through their thick skulls.

I'll give anything to keep her safe, even my life without a second thought.

"Put this on your head, and she will get to our destination safely," the man says, handing me a fabric sack.

I hesitate for a second, and he starts yelling, saying he will hurt Quinn if I don't comply.

I don't have much of an option.

Praying, I put the sack on my head, and all I can see is darkness. I hold on to Quinn's leg so that I know she's still there right next to me. I don't think I've ever been so scared in my life. My daughter wakes to all the noise, but luckily goes back to sleep, completely unaware of the danger we are in.

I want to cry and scream, but it's not going to help me right now. I need to think and stay calm. I have no idea where they are taking us, or why they targeted us. I don't care what I have to do to make sure it happens, but I'm going to find a way to survive this.

Or at least make sure my daughter does.

## Chapter Twenty-Seven

The car comes to a stop and I'm told I can remove the sack. When I do, I see that we are parked in a garage now. It's a small space, just enough to fit in two cars, and that's about it. I wonder who lives here.

"Take her and come inside," the woman says. She's obviously running the show, and is the mastermind behind this whole plan. She's going on her emotions, which makes me think this is personal. "And if you try to run, we will shoot you down."

I don't know what kind of monster would harm an innocent baby, but I know people like that are out there. I don't get what a young woman and man would benefit from it.

Revenge.

It must be.

The garage door is closed, so there's nowhere for me to run anyway. I could try to open it, but I wouldn't make it out in time. With my baby in my arms, I don't want to do anything reckless, but I might have to if it increases my chances of getting out of here alive.

"Can you tell me what you want?" I ask as I get out of the car, Quinn held against my chest. With one of them in front of me and one behind me, we walk inside the house, which seems to be well kept, tidy and normal, from what I can see. Nothing out of the ordinary at all.

Nothing makes sense.

"We will," the woman replies, gesturing for me to sit down on the couch. I do so, cradling my daughter. There is anger and hate in her eyes, and it's all directed at me.

"Do you have something against the Knights?" I ask, trying to figure out why she hates me so much.

Is that why I'm here? Or did my uncle do something and they found out that tie?

*Why am I here?*

"No, I don't. I have something against you," the woman says, snarling. "You have no idea, do you? You ruined my life. Because of you, my mother killed herself, because she couldn't live with the guilt over your father's death. And you sit there all happy, enjoying your life with your family. If I don't have my family, why should you have yours? My dad is in prison because of you. You've fucked up my entire world, and now you're going to pay for it."

Mother?

"Anne?" I guess.

It must be. Jean spoke of her college-age daughter, which fits the woman in front of me. In an alternate universe, Anne could have been my stepsister. Yet here she is, trying to hurt me and my family.

But I'm not going to stand for it.

I've been through too much and fought so hard to be where I am right now, and there is no way in hell I'm going to give that up.

"So you know who I am." She smirks, starting to pace up and down. "She was all that I had, you know. Her and Jasper. He wasn't a perfect dad, but he was there for me. And now because of you, she is gone forever, and my dad is rotting behind bars."

"Your mom made her own decision. It had nothing to do with me," I say, brows drawing together. "And Jasper is a criminal who killed my father. Behind bars is where he's meant to be."

She starts yelling at me. "This is all your fault! And you can't just get away with this! If I have to suffer, then so should you."

Her eyes are wide, and her fists are clenched. She basically has steam coming out of her ears. I don't know how she has justified blaming this all on me when it was her parents' own decisions that led them to where they are now. I guess everyone needs someone else to blame, but this is taking it to a whole new level. She's going to be following Jasper's footsteps and heading straight to prison.

The man who I assume is her boyfriend tries to calm her down. I'm hoping he has more sense than her, but she's obviously gotten him to go along with this whole thing, so maybe not. "It's okay, Anne. You will get your revenge. Don't let her get to you."

"Imagine the amount of people who are going to come after you if you harm me, or especially my daughter," I say, gritting my teeth. "The Knights of Fury MC won't give up until you're both dead. And do you even know who my uncle is? I also have a powerful family. Have you thought any of this through?" I don't care that I'm spilling secrets. They need to know the people who will come after them.

Do I feel bad her mom committed suicide? Sure. It's not nice for anyone to lose a parent and their support system. However, this blood is not on my hands.

I know it won't be long until Crow is here. I just need to make sure these two don't freak out and do something rash, like hurt me and Quinn. I slowly look around for a weapon of some kind, or anything I can use to defend myself.

I'm just thankful Quinn went back to sleep. Her cries definitely wouldn't have helped the situation any.

Anne shows no emotion, like she doesn't care who the Knights are, and I wonder just how well researched this whole thing was. She's obviously not thinking rationally, and she just wants to lash out at me not caring about the consequences. That makes her dangerous. "You have no idea what you've done, do you?"

The man starts looking a little nervous. He obviously isn't here for personal revenge—he just wants to support his girlfriend. "I know who the Knights are. Fucking hell, Anne, you didn't tell me that she was with one of them."

Hope fills me.

"I didn't know, but who cares? It doesn't change

anything. She is still the reason I've lost my mom. It doesn't matter who she knows," she says, scowling. "And if you love me and want to be with me, you'll stick to the plan. Now watch her while I go and get the gun. I'll make it fast and painless."

How kind of her.

She leaves and I start in on the weakest link here. With my daughter in my arms I can't physically fight, but words can be a weapon, too.

"If you hurt us, they're going to kill you both. Is that worth it for you? This isn't even your battle. You said you've heard of the Knights, then you'll know how severe the repercussions will be. My daughter's father is a club member. What do you think they will do to you both if either of us are harmed?"

He shifts on his feet, eyes darting all over the place. "My older brother, he just started prospecting for the Knights. He's going to kill me if he knows I'm involved in this. I don't know what to do. He already thinks I'm a fucking disappointment."

Shit. I didn't see that one coming.

I've met the three new prospects, and what are the chances that his brother ended up being one of them?

If this were my brother, I would be highly unimpressed too.

"You need to get us out of here unharmed," I whisper-yell to him. "Do you realize they will be on their way now and your brother could be with them? Don't ruin your life for a woman you won't even end up being with."

"Fuck," he curses, covering his ears with his

hands, like that is going to help the situation. "Okay, I need to think. Fuck. Come on then, I just want this over with now."

I stand and follow him to the front door, glancing behind me to make sure Anne isn't there with her gun. The last thing I want is to be shot in the back.

We reach the door and he pulls it open, and to my surprise and happiness, there stand Crow, Temper, Saint, Renny and Dee, guns in their hands, ready to fuck shit up.

"Fucking hell," Crow whispers as he pulls me into his arms, and turns around, covering us with his body.

"Take her," I tell him, passing him Quinn, needing to breathe and calm down. I brace myself on my knees for a moment. My daughter is going to be fine. I'm going to be fine.

We did it.

Temper grabs the boy and points a gun at his back.

"She's in there. Anne. She's Jean's daughter," I say to them. "She has a gun. And him. He was going to let me go. Don't hurt him. His brother is one of your new prospects."

I feel like I'm going to faint, my breath catching, as the reality of the situation hits me at full force.

I almost lost my daughter today.

And it wasn't because of the Knights, or my drug king uncle. It was because of me.

Crow holds on to me by one arm and pulls me to the car. "Are you okay? You're both safe now."

"I will be. My car is in the garage," I say, and he nods. "What are they going to do with them?"

"I don't know," he replies, buckling us both in the car. He grabs my face and looks into my eyes. "I fucking love you. They're lucky that you're okay, because if not..."

"I love you too. I knew you'd come for me."

"I'll always come for you."

"What's going to happen to the boy?" I ask.

"Don't worry, Bronte, we will sort it," he promises, getting in the front seat, and driving us away.

Relief fills me.

Crow would have made it inside before Anne got to me, but even if he didn't, I would have gotten out of there anyway. That guy would have opened the door and I would have run for my life, gone next door, done anything I had to to make sure my daughter was safe.

The other men stay behind, and I don't know exactly what they do, but Anne gets arrested. Her boyfriend, Smith, does too. Crow tells me that by pinpointing Smith as the weak link and using that, I saved myself and Quinn.

"You used your intelligence to make him an ally and to save yourself and our daughter. You bought yourself the time that you needed. Sometimes the heroes aren't the ones with the big muscles and guns, babe. Sometimes they are the ones with brains and courage."

God, I love this man.

Temper drives my car home, and the first thing I do when I get there is take a shower and cry.

I don't know what I would have done if I lost my daughter. Without her, I wouldn't even want to be in this world, and just the pressure and responsibility of being the one to protect her… If I'd made a wrong move, she could have died and that would have been on me.

It's heavy.

"I'm never leaving the house again," I tell Crow when I resurface. "Or maybe you should get me a few bodyguards to follow me and Quinn around. Also, I would like a few trained dogs—maybe some German shepherds?"

"Come here," he murmurs, wrapping me in his arms. "I've never been as scared in my life as I was today. My God, Bronte. If I had lost you both, that would have been my whole fucking world destroyed. You can have anything you want, I'm just happy that you're here, unhurt. I can't believe this happened. It just goes to show we need to always be careful, not only when there is some drama going on, but always. I think the dogs and guards are a good idea, or even if one of the brothers comes with you whenever you're going out alone. I'm not letting this happen again. I'm not going to lose either of you."

I start crying again, and this time, he cries with me.

Out of everything I've been through, this has been the worst. I don't care what life has to throw at me, but bring my baby into the picture and it takes it to a different level.

Having a child is like having your heart outside of your body, and it makes you vulnerable, both weaker and stronger.

Nothing ever fully prepares you for that.

## Chapter Twenty-Eight

I don't go anywhere by myself for the next week, and I know I'm being ridiculous, but I'm being cautious. While I still can't believe something like this happened to me, I know I did everything I could to protect my daughter. I'd do it all again. But that doesn't mean I want to leave my house.

"Come on, we're going out for a drink," Cam demands when she comes over, sick of my shit. "Now."

There's determination in those blue eyes, and I know she's not going to give up.

"I don't want to go out for a drink. Who is going to watch Quinn? Crow is—"

"On his way home right now and he's going to be with her. Come on, Bronte, let loose a little. Get your ass in the shower and put some makeup on. We're going back to Kamikaze for more margaritas," she says, doing a little shimmy dance move. "And we're going to do a dirty grind on the dance floor. You can show me those moves of yours."

I pout, considering her offer. "Can we get food afterwards?"

"That's a given."

"Fine," I groan, looking over at Quinn. "See the things your auntie makes me do?"

"Yeah, like have fun," Cam says to her. "And when you're old enough, I'll take you out to have fun, too."

"Where to? The nursing home?" I tease, running into the bathroom as Cam throws her shoe at me. I have a quick shower and throw on one of my little black dresses, some hoop earrings and block heels, then listen to Cam and add some makeup, a little lipstick, mascara and eyeliner.

"Can you do my hair?" I call out to her, and she comes into the bathroom and helps me curl my hair into beautiful beach waves.

Crow sticks his head in, eyes widening as he checks me out. "You look amazing." He then lowers his tone and adds, "And I'm glad Saint and Renny are going to be at the club."

Cam rolls her eyes. "You're such a Neanderthal. She will be fine. And she can handle herself if any men get out of control, can't you, Bronte?"

I nod. "Yes, of course. We'll be fine."

I remember that Abbie and Sky have also been kidnapped. Maybe it's an initiation to become a Knight. I laugh to myself, because if I don't laugh, I'll probably cry.

"What are you laughing about?" Crow asks.

"Nothing," I say, waving my hand. "I just realized that Abbie and Sky and I were all kidnapped—it must run in the family, that's all."

Crow does not look amused, but Cam laughs.

Crow is such a good dad and I'm lucky to be able to leave the house without any worries, knowing she is being well looked after. I know not all parents have that luxury. He gives me a long, lingering kiss good-bye, and then Cam and I head off.

I know she wants to get me out of the house, and I appreciate that. To be honest, it will be nice to spend some time with her and the girls.

When we arrive at Kamikaze, Abbie rushes out to meet us. "You both look stunning," she says, taking my hand. "Come on, the place is packed, but we get VIP treatment."

She's right—we walk to the front of the line and they let us in.

I see Saint as soon as I step inside. He's sitting at one of the private tables, Sky on his right, a bottle of Grey Goose on the center of the table. He sees me and calls me over.

"Nice to see you," he says, offering me a seat.

*You look hot*, Skylar mouths to me, patting the spot next to her. So does she, her long red hair framing her pretty face. "I'm so glad you came out tonight. How have you been?"

"Not too bad," I reply, accepting the drink Saint offers me. "Cam insisted I get out of the house tonight."

"I'm glad." She smiles.

Temper, Renny and Izzy come and sit with us, and I find myself wishing Crow were here. Still, I make the best of my time out, dancing with the girls until my feet are sore and having a few drinks in the mix. At the end of the night, when Saint and Skylar say they are leaving and ask me if I want a lift, I take them up on it.

Quinn is fast asleep in her crib when I get home, and Crow is naked, spread eagle on our bed, also passed out. After sliding off my heels, I place them in the corner of the room and strip down, then climb on the bed and crawl up his body.

"How was your night?" he asks, eyes fluttering.

"Good," I reply, laying my head on his chest and smiling. "I missed you, though. You should have come out."

"I wasn't invited," he replies, grinning.

"Well, you should have come up with the idea and invited me then," I tease, kissing the side of his neck. "I did dance, though, so I might be a little sweaty."

"Is that why you woke me up? You want to get a little sweatier?" he asks, rolling me over to my back.

If I'm being honest, that's exactly why I woke him up. "Maybe."

Definitely.

And then Quinn starts crying, and reality sets in.

"I'll get her," Crow murmurs, kissing me once more, and makes a sound of frustration before getting out of bed, sliding on some boxer shorts and leaving the room.

After he settles her and returns, though, he kisses all the way down my body, and makes me come so good, I put a pillow over my face so my screams aren't too loud.

And then I ride him, covering his mouth with my hand to do the same.

* * *

The next morning, I decide to go and do some grocery shopping.

With Quinn.

This is the first time I'll be leaving the house alone
with her, but I'm feeling good about it. I did protect her last time, and I will protect her always. Besides, it's not like any of our enemies are loose on the
streets; they are all behind bars.

I put her in a carrier around my chest, leaving my
arms free, which makes me feel more in control.

I think it's the randomness of the situation that
had me so paranoid. How was I to know that a young
woman complimenting my baby was planning on kid-
napping us for revenge? However, I can't live my life
being suspicious of everyone. I can pay more attention to my surroundings and trust my gut if something doesn't feel right.

I stop for coffee on the way home, sitting in a café,
just me and my daughter people watching. Feeling
more confident, I realize I am in control. I've come a
long way since I was working with Nadia. I can't stay
at home forever, hiding from life. That's not who I am.

Smiling to myself, I take a deep breath and pick
up Quinn. Looking into her eyes, I say, "Your mom
is strong, and we aren't going to be hiding anymore,
are we?"

She grins.

When I get home, Crow is waiting for me, and
the house has been cleaned, which I find extremely

sexy about him. He just does what needs to be done without complaint.

"How did it go?" he asks, taking Quinn from me.

"It was just what I needed. I even went out for a coffee, and yeah. I'm feeling pretty good," I admit. "I'll go and grab the bags in the car."

"I've got it," he says, handing Quinn back and heading to the front, returning with his hands full of bags. "There's a lot of chocolate here."

"I know," I reply, smirking.

"Chocolate and baby stuff. Did you actually buy anything for lunch and dinner?" he asks, amusement filling his tone.

"Yes, I'm going to make a new recipe for us, actually," I say, and help him unpack all the groceries. "Do you have to go into work today?"

He shakes his head. "No, but tomorrow I have to go to the clubhouse. Prez wants me to go on a run with him, and it might be overnight. Do you want to call Cam or Abbie or someone to come stay with you? Or are you going to be okay staying here alone?"

I reply instantly. "I'll be fine alone."

"Are you sure?"

I nod. "Yeah, I'm sure. What does one do on a run anyway?"

Crow hesitates, and I know we never really speak about a lot of the things that go on with the club. We're a family now, though, so I think it's time he let me in a little. I'm not going to judge anything he does, as I'm not completely naïve and know what I've gotten myself into. Still, a little insider knowledge would be nice. Like where are they going? What are they going to do? Is he going to be safe?

"Basically we're going over to another chapter of ours to talk some business with them. They need our help, we come. And vice versa. I think they are having some problems with their usual gun dealers, and want us to help them by hooking them up with our own," he explains, watching my reaction very closely. "Then they'll throw a party. It always ends in a party."

"So lots of women throwing themselves at you all," I guess, my eyes narrowing.

He shrugs, but doesn't deny it. "Does it matter? I'm a taken man and I'm not interested in anyone else."

"I know that, but it's hard to picture you sitting there and having all these beautiful women trying to get your attention, even if it's not reciprocated," I mutter.

"You have nothing to say about the gun trade deals? All you heard is the party part, didn't you?" he asks, lip twitching. "Babe, you have nothing to worry about. I can't stop women from looking, but I can make sure they know flat out I'm not interested. I'm not an idiot. You're the love of my life, and I'm not going to fuck that up for anything, okay?"

I do know that and I do trust him, but there's always that tiny sliver of doubt. Nadia would say that's my rational brain trying to get a word in over the loud thumping of my heart, but I think it's just my deepest fears making themselves known.

"Okay, just be safe," I say, kissing his lips.

The next morning I'm feeling relaxed about being

home alone. I know Crow must have been worried about leaving me, even though I've assured him that I was fine.

And when he comes home with a German shepherd puppy in his hands, I can't contain my excitement.

Well played, Crow. Well played.

"Oh my God," I squeal, holding my arms out. "That is the cutest puppy I've ever seen in my life."

"You said you wanted a guard dog, so I got you this little guy. He's from a line of police dogs, and I met both of his parents. They have an amazing temperament, great with kids but also very protective and intelligent. We'll need to get him proper training, and he's going to need a shit load of exercise and mental stimulation, but I think he's the perfect addition to our family."

"He *is* perfect," I agree, holding him against my chest. He licks my face and I fall in love with him a little more. I know he won't be able to protect me now, but he's definitely going to keep me busy.

"And when he's big and fully trained, he's going to protect you whenever I'm not here," Crow promises, smiling. "He's going to be a big dog. I have his bed and food in the car. You just need to choose a name for him."

If he wanted to distract me while he was gone, he did just that. Between Quinn and a puppy, I'm definitely going to have my hands full, but also my heart.

"How about Ghost?" I suggest.

"Ghost it is," Crow says as he pats his head. "You look after your mom tonight, all right, Ghosty?"

Crow gets ready to leave, and I get Ghost settled in, sorting out his bed, blanket, toys and food bowls. He's a longhaired dog, so I make a note to buy a good brush and to look into puppy school.

Like when Quinn was born, everyone drops in to see Ghost, just as Crow leaves. I don't know if this was all planned out, but I kiss him goodbye and watch as everyone dotes on both Quinn and Ghost.

Again, well played.

# Epilogue

*Two Months Later*

"I'm going to miss you around here," I tell Crow, pouting. "Who's going to bring me lunch? And annoy me all day? And make me want to rip his clothes off in public?"

"The answer to that better be no one," he replies in a dry tone, grinning and giving me a quick kiss. "I know, babe. I'm going to miss you too. But Temper wants me at the new club, so that's where I need to be. Fast & Fury is running itself now, especially with you here. I'm needed elsewhere. I think we'll both be a bit more productive if we work apart for a few hours. Besides, I'll still bring you lunch and annoy you all day."

"Yeah, I know," I grumble, smiling up at him.

After moving Crow to Divine, Temper had his younger brother Trade take over Fast & Fury. I don't know Trade that well—he's not officially in the MC—but he comes around the clubhouse. It's not like he's a stranger. Besides, he's dating Izzy's sister, Ariel, who is a sweetheart.

Speaking of Trade, he steps into the garage. "Hey," he says when he sees the two of us.

"Hey, brother," Crow says to him, glancing down at me. "You know Bronte, she's the one who is going to keep this place from falling into madness."

"Nice to see you again," I say to Trade, taking his hand as he offers it for a shake.

"Likewise," he replies, grinning.

He's a good-looking man. Tall. Man bun. Muscled. I wouldn't have pegged him as being Temper's brother, because Trade is much prettier.

Chains is next to step into the garage, dressed in all black leather, his dark eyes scanning the room. The girls were right; he did come around with me. Well, as much as Chains can come around.

"Guess who's a new employee here?" he asks, grinning, flashing his straight white teeth.

I glance up at Crow, who failed to mention that part.

He simply shrugs. "Temper wanted more man power."

"He's not working with customers, right?" I ask, eyebrows rising.

Because if he is, we're going to lose some.

"Don't worry, I'll make sure he doesn't scare too many away," Cam says, smirking. I'm so grateful to have her working here with me—she's become such a good friend to me, and we've bonded over our grief from losing Billie.

I'm truly surrounded by some amazing people.

"At least no customers will be rude when he's around," I joke.

Cam wraps her arm around me. "Change is hard, isn't it? It's going to suck here without Crow. I've never not worked with him."

"Tell me about it, but at least we have each other."

Her blue eyes smile at me. "Exactly. We've got this."

And we do.

With everything that has happened, I've learned one thing, and that's that I'm strong.

Resilient.

Crow pulls me into a hug and kisses my forehead. When he touches me, and kisses me, I can feel the love pouring out of him.

He loves me with all that he has, and I love him back in every way I know how.

I was made to be right here—Crow's woman and Quinn's mommy—and everything that comes along with that.

And with him at my side, I will always come out on top.

\* \* \* \* \*

*Reviews are an invaluable tool when it comes to spreading the word about great reads.*
*Please consider leaving an honest review for this or any of Carina Press's other titles that you've read on your favorite retailer or review site.*

*For more information on books by Chantal Fernando, please visit her website at www.authorchantalfernando.com.*

# *Acknowledgments*

A big thank-you to Carina Press for working with me on this new series!

Thank you to Kimberly Brower, my amazing agent, for having my back in all things. We make a great team, always have and always will.

Brenda Travers—Thank you so much for all that you do to help promote me. I am so grateful. You go above and beyond and I appreciate you so much.

Tenielle—Baby sister, I don't know where I'd be without you. Thanks for all you do for me and the boys, we all adore you and appreciate you. I might be older, but you inspire me every day. When I grow up, I want to be like you.

Christian—Thank you for always being there for me, and for accepting me just the way I am. I always tell you how lucky you are to have me in your life, but the truth is I'm pretty damn lucky myself. I appreciate all you do for me and the boys. I love you.

To my three sons, my biggest supporters, thank you for being so understanding, loving and helpful. I'm so proud of the men you are all slowly becoming, and I love you all so very much. I hope that watching me work hard every day and following my dreams inspires you all to do the same. Nothing makes me happier than being your Mama.

And Chookie—No, I love you more.

And to my readers, thank you for loving my words. I hope this book is no exception.

## About the Author

*New York Times*, Amazon and *USA Today* bestselling author Chantal Fernando is thirty-three years old and lives in Western Australia.

Lover of all things romance, Chantal is the author of the bestselling books *Dragon's Lair*, *Maybe This Time* and many more.

When not reading, writing or daydreaming, she can be found enjoying life with her three sons and family.

*Now Available from Carina Press and
Chantal Fernando.*

New York Times *bestselling author of the
Knights of Fury MC series Chantal Fernando is
back with her most complicated hero yet. He may
be the epitome of cool, but this MC President isn't
called Temper for nothing...*

*Read on for an excerpt from*
Temper

"That man keeps staring at you," Sierra says under her breath, eyes on the cash register. "He's kind of sexy, in an 'I don't know if I'm going to give you the best orgasm of your life or kill you in your sleep' kind of way."

I don't bother looking up, because I already know exactly who she's talking about. Temper, President of the Knights of Fury MC, has been coming into our family-owned bar, Franks, for several years now. He's not a regular—in fact, the MC only passes through maybe once or twice a year—but he's not someone that's easily forgotten.

The last time he was here, he told me that he was now the president because his Prez had died, and he practically cried as he said it. When he asked me out, like he always does each time he is here, I almost caved.

Almost.

"Abbie," Sierra growls. "Pay attention, he's coming over here."

I glance up just as he stands in front of the bar.

"Abbie," he says with a nod, smiling. "How have you been?"

"Not too bad," I reply, taking in those brown eyes and shaved head. I'm not quite being honest. With my mom's declining health, I've had to take over Franks, and had to drop out of college to do so. I spend every day here or at home, helping her as much as I can. My younger sister, Ivy, helps too, but I insisted she stay in college, so she can't always be here.

One of us had to make a sacrifice, and I volunteered. She can still become something, get out of this small highway town and follow her dreams.

"Really? It's been about eight months since I've seen you, and that's all you have to say?" he asks, brow furrowing.

I wish I had something exciting to say, like maybe tell him about a vacation I went on, or a competition I won, anything really, but I have nothing.

"Just work," I explain, smiling sadly. "Mom's not well, so I've had to take over with running the place."

He nods, understanding reaching his eyes. "I see. So you and Ivy work here full time now? What about school?"

"I've had to put that on hold," I admit, and it hurts to do so. I've always wanted to be a lawyer, ever since I can remember, but now it looks like my life is going to be spent serving drinks. When I brought up the idea of selling the place to Mom, you would have thought I had asked her for a million dollars. Franks has been in our family for decades, and it's more than just a bar to her, it's our family legacy. "Hopefully next year or so I can go back."

Temper's lips tighten. "I know how important that is to you."

He's killing me. I can't believe he remembers. Last time he was here, in addition to him opening up to me about Prez, I had told him just how much I was loving my courses. He commented on my excitement over it, telling me it was cute, and he could see just how passionate I was about school. And now here I am, months later, admitting to him how I've basically dropped out to work full time.

"Whiskey?" I ask, changing the subject. The last thing I want to discuss with him is how my life is no longer going according to plan, and I'm here because I need to be. Mom didn't want me to drop out either, but there was no other option, and now I'm stuck.

I always do this. I'm the first to want to help, the first to volunteer myself up, and you know what they say—no good deed goes unpunished. I'm learning how true that is firsthand. It's not like my mom is helping the situation either; she's milking it by just lying around the house feeling sorry for herself. And yesterday she didn't even go to her doctor's appointment. She seems depressed, and it's almost like the roles have reversed and I'm now the parent, and it's a whole lot of stress for me. I wish she would take her health seriously—she did have a stroke—and be responsible. Her doctors have said she will make a full recovery so long as she puts in the work. It's hard running Franks and constantly worrying about her as well.

I'm going to go gray soon, I can feel it.

He nods, and I take the opportunity to distract myself. It's been a while since I've seen him, and he looks good. It's like the man doesn't age. He's tall, strong, and kind of mean looking, but he's been nothing but nice and respectful toward me. We kind of have a routine going every time we see each other. We chat, we flirt, he asks if he can buy me dinner, and I say no. He accepts that and leaves, until next time.

I don't know why I always say no anymore. The first time was a combination of him being a biker and feeling so much older than me. But the age thing doesn't bother me that much anymore. Truth is I've never said yes, to any man, to any date. I get asked out by people coming into the bar, but you don't have to be experienced to know what they are really looking for, and it's not a loving, long-lasting relationship. My experience is severely lacking, aside from prom and the mistake I made after it, and there's no saving me now. I'm going to be a spinster. Hopefully Ivy will give me some nieces and nephews I can claim as my own.

Temper places money on the table, with a huge tip, like he always does. "Seriously? Who tips that much?"

His lip twitches. "You can take yourself out to a nice dinner with it, since I know you're never going to let me take you out."

"You giving up that easily?" I tease, giving him

a flirtatious smile. I don't know where this sudden boldness is coming from, other than the fact that I don't want him to stop asking me out, and I've only just realized this.

I've never met another man like Temper, and I don't think I ever will. I see how people treat him, avoid him, and make sure not to challenge him. Hell, my own mother warned me to be friendly with him, but never too friendly. He has this air of menace about him, but over the years I've also seen how he treats his MC brothers like family, and he's always respectful, even to the people who work here. I've seen him vulnerable when he talked about his Prez... Hammer was his name, I think. He's never rude, or arrogant— to me, anyway—and he's always generous and polite. When he speaks to me, he always uses a humble, gentle tone, one that I've come to enjoy listening to. I know there is another side to him, and I can't help but want to get to know that more.

"It only took a few years of rejection," he jokes, lifting the whiskey glass to his lips. I don't think I've ever heard him make a joke before.

"Maybe this was the year I was going to say yes," I reply, clearing my throat. I don't know what's come over me, but I have the feeling like if I truly do want to take a chance and go on this date, it's now or never. I'm stuck here, in the same job, doing the same thing every damn day, and I deserve to have a little fun and do something reckless for once in my life. I've always been the good girl, the trusted daughter, and the responsible older sister, taking care of my family as much as I can, since my dad has never been around. I know his name, Cohen Pierce, and that he lives in California somewhere. But he wanted, and still wants, nothing to do with me, and that's fine. I've accepted that.

But what have I ever done for me? Other than college, which I had to drop out of anyway, I can't think of one single thing.

Temper lowers his glass and studies me, brown eyes filled with surprise and suspicion. "You want to go on a date with me? Why now?"

Shrugging, I lower my eyes to the counter before returning them to him. "Time for me to live a little."

Being safe hasn't gotten me anywhere in life.

Now that I've opened my mouth and said this, Temper looks like he doesn't know what to do. In fact, he looks slightly concerned. "You want to live a little, so you have decided to take me up on the date I've been dreaming about for the last…how many years exactly?"

"Five, I believe," I mutter, and clear my throat once more. "Yes, pretty much, unless you've changed your mind now?"

He smirks. "You're the most beautiful woman I've ever laid my eyes on. I don't think I've ever asked anyone out more than once in my life." He pauses, and then adds, "Actually I can't even remember the last time I asked anyone out, other than you."

That can't be right.

We see each other twice a year at the most, and he's sexy as hell, powerful, and I'm sure he has women throwing themselves at him. And as for me being the most beautiful woman he's ever laid eyes on....

I don't think I'm anything special.

I mean, I know I'm not completely unfortunate in the looks department. I have long dark hair, and a curvy body that most people would consider to be plus sized, and along with my amber eyes and heart-shaped lips, I do okay. Yet I don't think I ever expected to encounter such a compliment.

"I don't know how any of that can be true," I say, shaking my head. "But you can explain it all over dinner. I finish here at seven."

"Seven it is." He nods, flashing me a grin. "I'll be here early in case you decide to change your mind."

"I won't," I declare, moving to serve a new customer that walks in.

I don't know how today took this turn of events, but for the first time in a long time, I'm excited.

*Don't miss*
Temper *by Chantal Fernando,*
*available now wherever*
*Carina Press ebooks are sold.*
*www.CarinaPress.com*